C333382577

JOHN TORODE'S CHICKEN
and other birds

JOHN TORODE'S
CHICKEN
AND OTHER BIRDS

photographs
by Jason Lowe

Quadrille
PUBLISHING

The humble chicken (I believe humble is the right word for chicken, underrated another) is by far the most-consumed meat in the modern world. It is fast to grow, easy to keep, multi-functional (chickens lay eggs too, after all) and vegetarians aside, appeals to nearly every cuisine in the world as well as most religions.

On landing in Blighty in 1992 I was stunned that many cooks believed that British produce was inferior to French. Somehow the French had it all sown up with chickens, in fact every bird in every restaurant was French – quails, ducks, guinea fowl, even pigeons. Things have moved on a mighty amount since then and still, for me, the best poultry and game comes from Britain, so let's make the best use of it.

I have always believed that if you can roast a chicken you will survive. It's a simple skill that gives you freedom. Use a different stuffing, vary the side dishes and sauces, or take that bird, rub it with spices and cook it in a tagine – yes, it is still roasting, just in a different way. And if you swap the chook for a guinea fowl, pheasant or duck, the meal will be a little different again. Master the roast chicken and you will quickly come to understand your oven and your taste buds, and from there the world is your oyster.

I was very young when I made gravy next to my nanna in Maitland, just outside Newcastle, Australia. She cooked simply but with real confidence, the confidence that comes with knowledge and practice. Her repertoire (if you can call it that) was not huge and that is why she has always been an inspiration. She knew how to roast the perfect chook, she knew how to make soup (fabulous asparagus and chicken soup), she cooked celebration meals (roast ducks and various other birds) and great family stews and pies. Oh, those pies – I am still trying to get mine to taste as good. She also knew what to do with the bits that were left over: big sandwiches made with the cold meat, stuffing and gelatinous gravy; fritters, salads, soups and pasta. She was good, and I hope that with this book I am able to impart some of her confidence in the kitchen, so that you too can cook with ease.

Home cooking is very different from restaurant cooking. Restaurants use formulaic recipes and employ chefs who have been honing the same dish for years. Although some of the recipes in this book have featured on the menus of my restaurants, this is not a restaurant cookbook, it's a people cookbook. It starts with the basics, jumps around a little and moves onto more complex recipes and techniques. The aim is to give you the confidence to cook a bird with style, whether it be a humble yet delicious roast chicken or salt and pepper quail with sweet chilli sauce. My advice is to get joy from the basics first – learn them, do them well. Some recipes you will love and some you will not – we are all different and we all like different things. Except a roast chicken, that is. We all love, love, love the roast chicken!

BIRDS OF A FEATHER

Many birds these days are farmed and history suggests that domesticating birds for eating has been happening for thousands of years. They are easy to transport, so are easy to take to market, and should you have one male and a few hens it is not that difficult to breed your own flock and feed the family.

Before the advent of large farms producing young birds specifically for the table, a chicken's life was destined to be spent laying eggs. Whether or not to kill and cook one of the family's chickens would have been a difficult choice and the act was often restricted to celebratory meals. Usually the birds chosen had spent many years laying eggs, hence the expression 'a tough old bird'. Older recipe books therefore tend to concentrate on boiling, braising, stewing and pot-roasting chicken – all long cooking processes that break down the tough meat fibres and encourage absorption of flavours from the other ingredients. It is only in the modern world that recipes call for tender chicken breasts, and birds stripped of their skin to appease dietary concerns.

The edible avers are many so let's start by separating the domesticated from the wild. Poultry is domesticated. These are birds that can be fully farmed and grow and mature well in a controlled environment. They are easy to process and transport, have a decent shelf life and don't need to be matured after slaughter. Chicken and turkey are two examples – a fairly recent entry to the list is guinea fowl, which has been bred as a domesticated bird but will be very different should you be lucky enough to catch the real thing in the wild and eat it.

Game birds are those that have not been domesticated and still run wild. They also need to be matured for a time after slaughter as their meat is so dense and well structured.

The domestic chicken is now a super power, its breeds mostly a number or code on the side of a carton, not a name. Chicken breeders continue to try and perfect their breeds using all sorts of methods so the birds can grow quickly and produce huge yields at minimal cost. The success of the chicken and our appetite for it is, after all, down to cost and accessibility.

The domestic chicken is usually female and grows for between six and 20 weeks. The longer the birds live, the stricter the regulations that control their rearing. In general, in a supermarket, most will be six weeks old, whereas an organic bird can be up to 120 days old and free range birds usually somewhere in between. The layers do not start to lay eggs until they are 26 weeks old, so no chicken that you buy from the shops would have laid eggs. Roosters, the males, aren't that good eating, but used to be castrated to become capons – that process is now illegal.

The female's considered the better domestic bird because she has a good temperament (quieter and better behaved) and grows more evenly than the male – not too fast or too big, which would make the flesh tough. In free range farms roosters sometimes go a bit nuts and fight – blokes, hey.

These days ducks, turkeys, guinea fowl, and quails have all been domesticated and are farmed in huge quantities. The simple fact is that unless the bird sits on the list of wild ones to the right, they are farmed and available year-round. All wild birds, however, are seasonal.

The farming of birds is a sensitive subject to some but if you have been given the facts then it is up to you to make the choices. Britain as a nation consumes 800 million chickens per year – yes, that's lots of chooks, and we consume a lot more eggs than that. The space required for these birds is huge. As previously mentioned, most domesticated birds are females, so the hatcheries will dispose of most eggs with a male gene at the laying stage and, should the eggs chick, they are disposed of (macerated) unless they are to be kept for breeding stock. This is the same for all domesticated birds – chicken, turkeys, ducks, quails and guinea fowl.

Although not farmed, most game birds are now reared under controlled conditions specifically for shooting, a sport that raises serious amounts of cash. Let's get one thing straight here: should there not be any shooting, the majority of these birds would simply disappear from the landscape. But most of the pheasant, partridge and woodcock will have been bought to the land where they are to be shot as polts (chicks), having been corralled and fed until they are at an age when they can fend for themselves, giving a high survival rate.

Few people understand the cost associated with raising a game bird. Some birds cost ten times as much to rear and be ready for the guns as they sell for in the shops. So do buy a pheasant or partridge next time you see one –they are delicious, and it means they will get eaten.

GAME SEASONS

Grouse
12 August – 10 December
Ptarmigan
12 August – 10 December
Black Game
20 August – 10 December
Partridge
1 September – 1 February
Pheasant
1 October – 1 February
Snipe
12 August – 31 January
Woodcock
1 September – 31 January (Scotland)
1 October – 31 January (England & Wales)
Wild Duck and Geese
1 September – 31 January (inland)
1 September – 20 February (below high water mark)

BIRDS OF A FEATHER

CHICKEN

Today's commercial chickens are an amalgamation of various breeds, bred to grow quickly and produce the right amounts of soft flesh that we all love so much. You can still find some traditional breeds on sale in the UK and the Rare Breeds Survival Trust (www.rbst.org.uk) has a good list, but very rarely now do the Brits buy chickens according to their breed, mainly because there was no traditional breed that produced huge breasts (stop the giggling) and long fleshy legs. The French however prize some breeds and at the top of the table is the long-legged Poulet de Bresse, which has a very long, thin breast and a deep, almost gamey flavour.

DUCK

There are many types of duck. The short-necked mallards are those petrol-coloured birds many of us have thrown bread to on a Sunday afternoon. They are tiny compared to the Gressingham, which is a mighty duck that has trouble getting off the sofa. Gressinghams have massive breasts with a good amount of meat to fat. For me the real gem, however, is the Peking: long necked and white all over, it almost looks like a goose. These are the commercial varieties and when it comes to wild ducks the variation is so great it is almost unbelievable that they are the same species. The widgeon, for example, is a tiny duck that is almost pigeon.

GOOSE

The temperamental goose is a majestic bird. The females are bred for our tables as the males are little ruffians. Flocks of geese are said to be soul mates – should they get separated they suffer depression and stop eating and growing, so many farmers send a whole flock to slaughter at one time. Those mottled grey squawking things that inhabit parks are Canada Geese – their meat is okay, but not anywhere near the quality of farmed goose. Geese are bred in three categories: light, medium and heavy, mainly due to the amount of meat they produce. Most domesticated geese are light. The heavier the goose, the bigger the frame it will need to get off the ground; it will also carry a lot more fat.

GROUSE

This is where we start to see the difference between game birds and domesticated fowl in all their glory. Grouse is the most expensive bird by weight. Many people have tried to domesticate them but so far unsuccessfully and of this I am glad. They love cold weather, almost sub-arctic, and exist primarily in the northern hemisphere. Within the grouse family there are birds that can no longer be shot in the UK, such as black game and ptarmigans. This is really due to them having been over-shot and so difficult and expensive to breed and keep.

GUINEA FOWL

The domesticated guinea fowl is a shadow of its wild former self. Once a big, long-necked bird with a skinny body and quite a nutty flavour, the guinea fowl as we know it now has a thin skin and a tiny amount of (still nutty-tasting) flesh. The birds come in many colours, from coral to pearl to mottled lavender, but ultimately a guinea fowl is a guinea fowl is a guinea fowl. As with most fowl the females produce more meat.

PARTRIDGE

A member of the pheasant family, partridge is a game bird that is bred for shooting as sport. These birds are very expensive to keep but because those who shoot them pay so much for the honor, the partridge is not an expensive bird for the table. There are two varieties. The grey leg is spread all over the world, so is abundant and common. The red leg, sometimes referred to as the French partridge, is preferred on the European continent.

PHEASANT

The only real difference between pheasants these days is whether they are male or female. The male is slightly bigger, with strong legs and a frame that is sometime a little too big for the amount of meat that is produced. The hen has large breasts and skinny legs – a supper model, if you will. The males have a rich gamey flavour that I prefer but if you are looking for simple cooking and easy-to-carve breast, go for the hen.

PIGEON

Wood pigeon, Trafalgar square pigeon, wild pigeon, homing pigeon, French pigeon – there are thousands of breeds of pigeon but in reality few are suitable for eating and although pigeons are sometimes shot, most that we see on sale are bred. To make things very simple, there are two main varieties. Wild pigeons from Britain are small birds (not much bigger than quail) with dark meat. The French variety is plump and large with huge amounts of meat not just on the breast but also the legs – they are expensive but well worth it.

QUAIL

The quail is a land-dwelling bird scattered on different continents. It's not clear whether they originated in Africa or China. It's not just the birds themselves that are valued but their tiny, sweet and delicate eggs. Many of the quails we consume are a cross between an African and a blue Chinese bird, and again they are bred for yield. Very few could be termed game, however good quail has to have plenty of land to run around in, so it produces deep-flavoured sweet meat, fleshy legs and delicious little breasts.

TURKEY

The turkey is a non-flying bird from the US. American Indians loved its plumage and it has a place in Thanksgiving celebrations, though how it became the centrepiece of the Christmas table is difficult to trace. There are three main varieties. The white is the most common table bird for no reason other than the stubble from the plumage is not detectable when plucked and the birds therefore look cleaner. However some people believe that other breeds – particularly the black and the bronze – are gamier and that the whites are too similar in flavour to chicken. The bronze is considered the finest turkey with good-sized breasts but not the massive legs of the white or the black.

SHOPPING

When it comes to shopping the general rules are, in my mind, common sense. Try and buy from someone you know and buy a decent farm label rather than a generic, mass-produced factory brand. You will taste the difference between them – the factory brand will taste of almost nothing!

The skin of whole birds should be intact – there should be no tears in it at all – but the very worst thing is to find something that looks like a burn mark on the pointy part of the breast. This shows that the bird has been burned from the ground that it sits on and is not good at all.

Look for plump, healthy, clean, shiny birds with even colour under the skin. If there is a broken bone or a blood spot then stay clear. Blemishes indicate the bird has slipped through the control net or the farm is not looking after the birds well. However, if you have already cooked a bird when you discover a blood spot, just cut around it – it will not hurt you.

Also choose a bird that looks in proportion. I know that sounds a bit weird, but a chicken should not look scrawny, a duck should not look fatty, a pheasant should not be a big plump thing, and a turkey should not be round like a bowling ball – it should have the shape of a turkey.

I have already said birds grow fast and some farms take advantage of this. I think you should be looking for free range birds if you have the money, and I know not all of us do, but look at it this way: the longer a bird takes to grow, the less the meat will shrink when it is cooked. Birds that are forced to grow fast shrink like mad when cooked because they contain huge quantities of water.

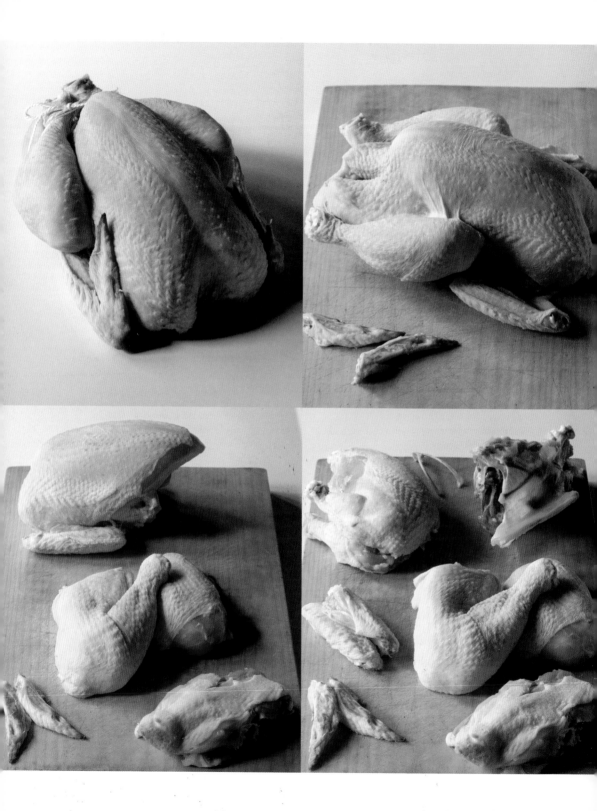

JOINTING A BIRD

A bird has a few bits to it, but fortunately all birds have the same bits. Some of the best are inside the bird and most prized is the liver. When buying a bird you will often find a plastic bag inside containing the offal and neck; these are great for making stock.

The hen of any bird has the plumpest breasts – nothing unusual there! The breasts are guarded by the wings and above that you will find the opening to the neck – remember: the wing end is the neck end; the other end is the cavity. Stuffing goes in the neck end, however you can put flavourings in the cavity.

It is much more economical to buy a whole bird, joint it yourself, and get the most out of it, rather than buying portions in a foam tray. Learning to joint a chicken is one of the most useful skills a cook can have and is easy with a bit of practice.

To do it, place the bird breast up on a board. Pull one wing out and slice through the joint half way down the wing – this is known as the chicken shank. Repeat on the other side.

Take each leg and remove the knuckle by cutting clean though the joint – you will be left with legs in the classic drumstick shape. With the parson's nose pointing towards you, take a leg in each hand – this needs to be a firm hold, not a flimsy attempt! Pull the legs away from the bird so that they stretch out but do not snap or tear the skin. Use the knife to cut the skin between the breast and the legs.

Pinch the skin at the cavity end together, holding it closed. Make a cut above the pinch but underneath the point of the breastbone and follow the breast line along to meet the cut you made above the leg. Repeat on the other side.

Hold the breast firmly from above with one hand. Pick the chicken up and rest it back on the wings and, with the other hand, pull the legs down firmly, snapping the backbone. Cut through the area where it naturally snapped. You now have a crown (the two breasts joined together on the bone) plus the legs and thighs attached to the backbone.

Take a leg in each hand, skin-side towards the board, and snap the legs towards each other – this dislocates the legs from the backbone. Cut each leg off at the thigh along the natural split.

Sit the crown so the wing joints face you and lift the skin to reveal the wishbone. Cut in between the flesh and the wishbone in a neat v-shape so that you can pull the wishbone out. Stretch the skin tightly across the top and mould the breast back into shape. Following the line of the bone, run the knife through to the bone and let the weight of the breast help it fall off the bone while you encourage its release with your knife. This is easiest using a quick flicking motion directed away from you.

When the breast has come away, hold it with the wing down and cut through the wing joint. Repeat on the other side and you are done.

HOW TO USE THE RECIPES

The recipes in this book are simple enough and should be easy for you to follow – I like them to be short and inspiring, rather than dictatorial.

The number of birds is an indication of portions and they are just an indication.

 means a dish should serve four people while means a dish will serve two to four people, depending on the size of the portions and how hungry you all are.

A few other points: when a recipe asks for 'salt and pepper', it assumes you are using freshly ground black pepper as a rule. However I often use other types of pepper instead and when these are required they will be specified in the ingredients list. When it's best to use flaky sea salt rather than granulated salt, the recipe will say so too.

Where a recipe says vegetable oil, you can use any light, neutral tasting oil; in these cases the flavour of olive oil will be too distinctive. If it's important to use extra virgin olive oil, the ingredients list will say so, but otherwise you can use pure or virgin olive oil if you have it.

All the tablespoon measures are 15ml and teaspoons 5ml, while the eggs are medium.

Some of the sauce and dressing recipes will produce more than you need for one day because it's often easiest to make a decent batch and have some leftovers on stand by for subsequent meals.

Please do remember that there are plenty of variables when it comes to food and cooking, from your oven to the size of your handful to how sharp your knife is.

My advice is to practice – pick a recipe and cook it not once, not twice, but four or five times. Get confident with it, feel it, and change or adapt it to suit your own taste. Don't think that when you cook everything should just work and if not the recipe is at fault. Concert pianists always make a mistake or two the first few times they play a new piece of music and it is only with practice, confidence and knowledge that you will become a great cook, regardless of the size of your repertoire. Remember my nanna, a great, great, great cook and still the best chook cook in the world.

The great soups of the world have never been made from scraps or leftovers as many people think. Great soups are made with the finest ingredients and are chock-a-block full of goodness. The Italians used to boil meats, serve the broth to the kings and queens, and then throw the meat to the peasants. For the great Jewish staple chicken soup a whole chicken is simmered so that all its flavour is extracted; the bird itself is dispensed with. Even for classic cream of chicken soup you should use only the very best. Don't skimp: buy quality, cook it carefully and you will have a good pot of soup that satisfies and heals.

Traditionally all chickens were kept for laying eggs and at the end of the yearly laying cycle became 'old boilers' – these made the best stock. There are two basic types of chicken stock: brown chicken stock, where the bones are roasted before simmering, and white chicken stock, which is more common. The liquid chicken stock and stock cubes you buy from a supermarket will have a white chicken stock flavour. Many people use the bones leftover from roast chook for stock making. Although the bird has been roasted the result will be almost like white stock because the bones themselves have not been coloured.

soups & stocks

CLASSIC CHICKEN STOCK

MAKES ABOUT 4.5 LITRES

1 whole chicken, split down
   the centre and rinsed under
   cold water
2 carrots, peeled
1 leek, split lengthways
some herb stalks
2 bay leaves
2 cloves
10 black peppercorns
a little salt

This recipe uses a whole chicken. You could use chicken bones instead, but they won't give the best flavour.

Put everything in a really big pot and add about 5 litres of cold water. Bring slowly to the boil, then reduce the heat to a simmer and cook for 2 hours.

Remove the pot from the heat and leave the stock to cool overnight. Next day, bring the stock slowly to the boil again, then remove from the heat, allow to cool slightly and strain the liquid through a clean tea towel into a large bowl.

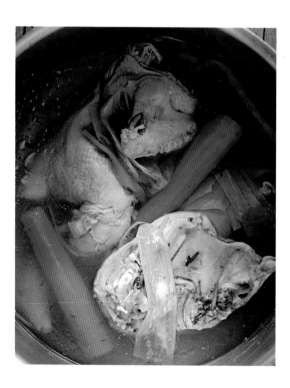

GAME STOCK

MAKES ABOUT 2 LITRES

1kg bones from game birds,
  such as pheasant, partridge,
  guinea fowl – whatever you
  have – including necks and
  wings
vegetable oil
1 onion
1 leek
¹/₂ fennel bulb
1 stick celery
1 carrot
¹/₄ cabbage
2 garlic cloves
1 handful herbs such as
  parsley, chives, sage and
  basil, including the stalks
1 star anise
10 black peppercorns, crushed
a little salt
1 handful ice-cubes

Heat the oven to 220°C (gas 7). Chop the bones so that they are roughly the same size as the palm of your hand. Put them in a heavy roasting tray and mix with a little vegetable oil. Roast for a good 40 minutes or until well coloured all over, moving them once during cooking.

While the bones are roasting, cut all the vegetables and garlic into 2.5cm chunks, keeping the cabbage separate. In a large casserole, gently sweat the onion, leek, fennel, celery, carrot and garlic in a little oil until soft, keeping the pot covered and making sure the vegetables do not colour.

Drain the bones of any excess oil then add them to the vegetables in the casserole. Pour in 4 litres of cold water and add the cabbage, herbs, spices and salt, and place over the heat. Throw in the ice cubes, which will set the fat and make a raft form on the surface of the liquid. Skim it off, then bring the stock to the boil and keep skimming off any fat that settles on the surface.

After 10 minutes of constant skimming, turn the heat down so the stock is barely moving and leave it to cook for 3 hours.

Remove the casserole from the heat and allow the stock to cool with all the ingredients still in the pot. Strain the liquid, ensuring you squeeze all the juices from the vegetables and bones. The stock should be reasonably clear, brown in colour and very flavoursome.

CREAM OF CHICKEN SOUP

SERVES 🐔🐔🐔🐔🐓🐓

1.2 litres chicken stock (page 20)
100g butter
100g flour
200ml milk
100ml cream
salt and white pepper

Ah, the classics are always the best, and cream of chicken soup is a beauty. It keeps well and is as simple as anything to make. If you are a purist, then the stock should be home-made, but if you want to taste it as many a child has done, then a few stock cubes will work too. For a fancy version, add a pinch of fresh tarragon, or strips of chicken. On a cold day, a little cream of chicken soup with hunks of buttered bread, or even buttered toast dropped into it, is yummo-scrummo.

Bring the stock to the boil in a saucepan. Meanwhile, in a separate saucepan – a large, heavy-based one – melt the butter over a lowish heat, then add a good pinch of white pepper and some salt. Let the butter start to bubble, then add the flour and reduce the heat. This is where you need to keep stirring: the mix (or roux as it is called) will slowly turn white.

Start slowly ladling the stock into the pan of roux, stirring the mixture as it starts to boil. I mean really stir – and keep on stirring as you add more stock so that there are no lumps. (There is a trick you can use with a food processor if you do have lumps but do try to stir them out.)

When all the stock has been added, return to the boil and add the milk. Taste the soup and season – it should taste of chicken. If it doesn't, then add some stock cube or concentrated chicken stock – but not gravy granules as they will turn it brown. When you are ready to serve, add the cream and away you go.

CHICKEN AND ASPARAGUS SOUP

SERVES

100g butter
30 large asparagus spears
2 potatoes, peeled and diced
2 leeks, trimmed and diced
2 shallots, diced
1.5 litres chicken stock (page 20)
extra virgin olive oil, for
  sprinkling
salt and pepper

Soup – made with whole asparagus? Are you sure? What about the cost? Yes, yes, yes. You can't make a silk purse from a pig's ear: the best soups are made with the finest ingredients. We snub soup, for some strange reason, as cheap food, but that shouldn't be, and this one – seasoned properly, finished with some fabulous olive oil, then savoured with really fresh bread – is fantastic.

Melt the butter in a large, heavy-based saucepan over a low heat. Snap the asparagus stems from their tough bases and add the tough part to the butter. Season generously with salt and pepper. Add the potatoes and leeks, and cook for 2 minutes, then add the shallots and cook for a further 4 minutes.

Stir in the stock, bring to the boil and cook over a medium heat for 15 minutes or until the potato is soft. Transfer the soup to a food processor and whizz to a fine purée.

Strain the soup through a fine sieve into a clean saucepan, pushing all the flavour from the fibrous remains, which you should then discard. Gently reheat the soup.

Cut the asparagus spears in half so you have 30 tips about 5cm long – these will be your garnish, so cook them in a pan of boiling water for 4 minutes. Add the rest of the stalks to your soup pan and cook for the same amount of time.

Blend the soup until smooth once more. To serve, pour into six bowls, garnish with the cooked asparagus tips and sprinkle with a little extra virgin olive oil.

Tip: this soup is great with croutons. To make them, cut some stale bread into bite-size chunks and put them on a tray in the oven – don't add oil. Turn the oven to 170°C (gas 3) and cook for 15 minutes, or until coloured.

CHICKEN SOUP
WITH MATZO BALLS

SERVES

1 large boiling fowl or old
  chicken
salt
3 carrots
2 onions
1 stick celery
1 tsp peppercorns
3 eggs
1 handful chopped parsley

MATZO BALLS
10 large matzo crackers
1 onion, finely diced
a little vegetable oil
2 eggs
a little matzo meal
1 pinch grated nutmeg
salt and pepper

Yes – here you use a whole chicken and don't eat the meat. This recipe is all about the goodness of the broth, the flavour of the soup and the great matzo balls. The 'golden egg' is an egg that is still inside a female chicken and is the prize of any Jewish family soup pot. To be a little PC (unusual for me, I know), I float boiled egg yolks in the soup instead.

Chop the chicken into 12 pieces. Put these in a pot of cold water, add some salt and leave to soak for 20 minutes, then throw the water away (this washes off the blood and stops the soup being cloudy).

Put the chicken in a soup pot with the vegetables and peppercorns. Add enough water to cover the chicken by 10cm. Bring to the boil, then reduce the heat and simmer for 5-6 hours, topping up the water if it goes below the top of the chicken.

Meanwhile, in a large saucepan, boil the eggs for 8-10 minutes. Drain and leave to cool in cold water. Peel off the shells and remove the whites, leaving the cooked yolks whole. Set aside.

Strain the broth and season as needed. Take out 200ml of broth to use when cooking the matzo balls and put it in a saucepan.

Leaving the matzo crackers in the sealed plastic they come in, crunch them up into little pieces. Open the pack and drop them into a bowl of water, but strain immediately.

Fry the onion in the oil without letting it colour. Put the cooked onion in a bowl and add the rest of the ingredients, mixing to a paste and adding more matzo meal if needed. Roll into marble-sized balls. Drop the balls into the reserved broth, bring to the boil and cook for 15-20 minutes.

Combine both broths, the matzo balls and hard-boiled egg yolks in a large tureen and scatter with chopped parsley to serve.

STRACCIATELLA

SERVES

1.5 litres chicken stock (page 20)
3 skinless chicken breast
    fillets, cut into strips
4 eggs
60g parmesan cheese, grated
1 large handful parsley, finely
    chopped
ground black pepper

The important thing with this soup is to take it from the heat as soon as you have added the egg mixture or it will overcook. The egg, parmesan and parsley will float to the top like a raft, leaving the rich stock and chunks of chicken sitting below. Fresh stocks are readily available on supermarket shelves if you don't want to make your own, and if push comes to shove you can use a stock cube.

Place a saucepan over a high heat, pour in the stock and bring to the boil. Add the chicken strips to the boiling stock and cook for 5 minutes.

Meanwhile, in a small bowl or jug, beat the eggs with the cheese, chopped parsley and black pepper.

Pour the egg mixture into the boiling liquid and remove from the heat immediately. Divide the soup among six large bowls and serve with good bread and butter or olive oil.

CHICKEN AND ASPARAGUS CHOWDER

SERVES

100g butter
1 large onion, roughly chopped
2 large celery sticks, roughly chopped
1 garlic clove, roughly chopped
500g asparagus, roughly chopped
1 bay leaf
100g plain flour
2 litres chicken stock (page 20)
2 cooked chicken breasts, shredded
50ml double cream
salt and white pepper

Melt the butter in a large saucepan. Add the onion and celery, and some salt and pepper. Cook for 5 minutes without colouring. Add the garlic and asparagus and continue cooking for 2 minutes. Season again, add the bay leaf and flour, and give the pan a good stir. Continue cooking for another 2 minutes, stirring often.

Pour in the stock and bring to the boil. Skim off any funny bits and give the bottom of the pan a good scraping. Simmer for about 15 minutes then take the pan off the heat. Lift out the bay leaf and transfer the soup to a food processor. Blend until smooth.

Return the soup to the saucepan and bring to the boil. Taste and season as you like. Drop in your shredded chicken and bring the soup back to the boil. Stir in the cream off the heat and serve.

Variation: You can replace the asparagus with two large cans of sweetcorn kernels, drained. In that case, simply blitz the soup rather than purée it.

PUMPKIN AND CHICKEN SOUP WITH BEANSPROUTS AND CORIANDER

SERVES

300ml vegetable oil
50g fresh chillies, thinly sliced
50g garlic, thinly sliced
50g shallots, thinly sliced
100g red curry paste
30g palm sugar
1 large butternut squash,
    peeled and cut into 4cm
    chunks
2 x 400ml cans coconut milk
175ml coconut cream
1 tbsp Thai fish sauce
2 tbsp lime pickle
3 lemongrass stalks, crushed
4 chicken breast fillets, cut
    into strips or chunks
500g precooked mung bean
    noodles or egg noodles
100g fresh beansprouts, picked
1 small bunch coriander,
    picked

Adding lime pickle was a last-minute thing when I first made this dish – I wanted a little more piquancy and spice. Normally I wouldn't add an Indian flavour to a Thai recipe, but the result is fragrant, sweet, sour, hot and salty, with all the flavours taken up by the rich, floury noodles. The fried garnish is optional.

Heat the oil in a wok and add the sliced chillies. Cook slowly over a gentle heat until all the moisture from the chillies has evaporated (at which point the oil will stop bubbling), then raise the heat slightly, so that they caramelise and crisp up – without turning too dark. Remove and repeat the process with the garlic, then the shallots. Set them all aside.

Drain off all but 80ml or so of the oil. Add the red curry paste to the wok and fry for 2 minutes, then add the palm sugar and let it cook with the curry paste for 4 minutes, until sticky and fragrant. Add the butternut squash, stir well and cook for 2 to 3 minutes.

Pour in the coconut milk and coconut cream, then add the fish sauce, lime pickle and lemongrass. Bring to the boil and cook for 20-30 minutes over a medium heat until the squash is soft but not mushy. Add the chicken, return to the boil and cook for 5 minutes but no longer.

Put your precooked noodles in a bowl and pour boiling water over them to reheat. Leave for 2 minutes, then drain. Divide the noodles among serving bowls and add a few pieces of squash per portion. Pour in the remaining soup and garnish with the fried chillies, garlic and shallots, plus the beansprouts and coriander.

CHICKEN SOUP
WITH COCONUT MILK

SERVES

1 small bunch coriander with roots

2 chicken breast fillets, about 125g each, sliced lengthways

1 litre thin coconut milk, plus 250ml thick coconut milk

2 stalks lemongrass, bruised and cut into 2.5cm pieces

8 thick slices galangal, peeled

10 lime leaves, torn

4 small green chillies, crushed in a mortar

4 tbsp fish sauce

4 tbsp lime juice

Coconuts grow in abundance in the south of Thailand and the milk extracted from their flesh is used for everything. This soup (tom kha gai) should hold a lot of spice, as the number of chillies indicates, because of the coconut milk's natural sweetness. This recipe serves four as a starter or six to eight people as part of a full Thai meal.

Separate the coriander leaves from the stems. Set the leaves aside and crush the roots and stems together in a mortar.

In a large saucepan, combine the chicken, thin coconut milk, lemongrass, galangal and crushed coriander roots and stalks. Bring to the boil and simmer for 4 minutes.

Add the lime leaves and chillies, then stir in the thick coconut milk. Return the mixture to the boil. Immediately take it off the heat and add the fish sauce and lime juice. Taste and correct the seasoning if necessary. Serve the soup garnished with the reserved coriander leaves.

CHICKEN & GALANGAL SOUP

SERVES

2 chicken breast fillets, about
   125g each, cut into fine strips
5 thick slices galangal
2 stalks lemongrass, bruised
   and cut into 2.5cm pieces
3 coriander roots, bruised
6 small green chillies, crushed
   in a mortar
2 large red chillies, deseeded
   and cut into small pieces
3 tbsp fish sauce
3 lime leaves, torn
4 tbsp lime juice
10 Thai basil leaves

Although similar to the famous Thai soup tom yum, this simple recipe has a more delicate flavour that is the result of cooking the chicken in water. Stock would be too strong here, its flavour overpowering. This recipe serves four as a starter, or six to eight people when served as part of a full Thai meal.

Put the chicken in a large saucepan and cover with 1 litre of cold water. Bring to the boil and add the galangal, lemongrass, coriander roots and all the chillies. Simmer for 4 minutes.

Add the fish sauce and lime leaves, then taste and adjust the seasoning as necessary. Remove the saucepan from the heat and add the lime juice and Thai basil leaves before serving.

YUGOSLAVIAN CHICKEN SOUP WITH SPÄTZLE

SERVES 🐔🐔🐔🐔🐔🐔🐔🐔

1 whole chicken
2 potatoes
3 parsnips
2 onions
a load of parsley stalks, plus a
  large handful chopped
  parsley leaves
salt and pepper

SPÄTZLE
100g plain flour
1 egg
1 tbsp warm milk

Spätzle are simply a type of noodle, but when making them it is helpful to have a spätzle pan, which is like a tray with holes drilled in it. Alternatively, you can use a piping bag fitted with a small nozzle to make the dough look like short worms.

Yugoslavians tend to thicken their soups by including lots of potato in the broth, which makes the spätzle a bit obsolete in my opinion, so I use far less potato than some may say is authentic – sorry.

Put the chicken in a big pot, cover with water, add a good handful of salt and place over the heat. After 20 minutes throw the water away.

Peel and finely dice the potatoes, parsnips and onions, and add them to the pot with the parsley stalks, some salt and pepper, and more water to cover. Bring to the boil then reduce the heat and simmer gently for 5 to 6 hours.

Strain the stock and skim off the fat. Cut the breast meat from the chicken and shred it. Put half the stock in a saucepan with the breast meat and use the rest of the stock to cook the spätzle.

Mix all the spätzle ingredients together to form a batter, adding a pinch of salt to the flour. Bring the reserved stock to the boil in a large saucepan. Push the dough through a spätzle tray if you have one, or squeeze it through a piping bag fitted with a small nozzle and cut into matchstick lengths.

Drop the little noodles into the boiling stock – they take about 2 minutes to cook. Lift them out with a slotted spoon or similar and plunge them into cool water.

Add the parsley leaves to the soup, then the spätzle and stir well before serving.

GAME CONSOMMÉ
WITH GAME DUMPLINGS

SERVES

CONSOMMÉ

1 carrot, peeled and cut into
   chunks
1 stick celery, cut into chunks
1 shallot, peeled and cut into
   chunks
a few sprigs of parsley
100g minced chicken
200g minced pork
2 egg whites
4 ice cubes, crushed
2 litres good-quality game
   stock, plus 400ml-450ml
   extra for cooking dumplings
   (page 21)
salt and pepper

DUMPLINGS

50g chicken, duck or other
   poultry livers
200g flour
50g suet

GARNISH

4 pheasant breast fillets
1 handful chervil leaves
truffle oil

**I like this rich, livery soup. The dumplings are delicious
and add that richness that the game deserves.
Consommé needs great stock – this is one of those
times when you really should make your own.**

To make the consommé, put the carrot, celery, shallot, parsley
and some salt and pepper in a food processor and blend until the
vegetables are finely chopped. Add the minced meats, egg whites
and ice, and blend again.

In a large pot, stir the stock and meat mixture together. Place
over a low heat and cook slowly until the meat mixture floats to
the top to form a raft. Increase the heat and let the pot simmer
gently for 30 minutes (do not let it boil). Turn off the heat and
leave the consommé to sit – never stir it.

To make the dumplings, put the livers, flour, suet and a little salt
and pepper in a food processor and blend until smooth. Roll the
dough into hazelnut-sized balls and chill.

Heat the oven to 180°C (gas 4) and put an ovenproof frying pan
over a medium-high heat. In a wide saucepan, bring your extra
400-450ml of stock to a simmer. Rub the pheasant breasts
generously with oil and lots of salt and pepper. Sear the breasts
in the frying pan, giving plenty of colour to the skin and
underside, then transfer to the oven for 15 minutes. Drop the
dumplings in the stock and cook for 20 minutes.

Meanwhile, strain the consommé gently – preferably through a
muslin cloth, but most important is that you do it slowly. Remove
the pheasant from the oven, let it rest for 5 minutes, then slice
thickly. Put some dumplings in each serving bowl, pour in the
consommé, then scatter with chervil and a few drops of truffle
oil. Serve each bowl with a few slices of pheasant alongside.

GAME BROTH
WITH PEARL BARLEY

SERVES 🐔🐔🐔🐔

1 large onion
1 large carrot
1 turnip
2 small partridges, breasts and
  legs removed
800ml game stock (page 21)
1 tbsp pearl barley
1 large handful chopped
  parsley
flaky sea salt and pepper

Yes, a good hearty, wintry soup that is a meal all on its own. It is best, in my opinion, to make this a few days before you want to eat it – the flavour just gets better and better.

Peel the vegetables and cut them into dice about the size of your little fingernail.

Put the partridge legs, stock and chopped vegetables in a heavy-based casserole over a medium heat and bring to a simmer. Add the pearl barley and adjust the heat so that the liquid barely simmers (should it boil, the vegetables will break up) and leave to cook, uncovered, for 20 minutes.

Preheat the oven to 180°C (gas 4). Lay the partridge breasts on top of the soup and transfer to the oven for 1 hour.

Remove the casserole from the oven. Lift out the legs and strip the meat from the bones, chopping it very finely. Cut the breasts into small dice. Return the meat to the soup and season to taste with a heaped teaspoon of sea salt and a good amount of pepper. Stir in the parsley just before serving with lots of hot bread.

CHINESE DUCK SOUP WITH NOODLES

SERVES

1 Chinese roast duck (page 174)
1 carrot, roughly chopped
1 celery stick, roughly chopped
1 large onion, roughly chopped
1 leek, roughly chopped
5cm piece root ginger, peeled
  and sliced
6 star anise
1/2 tsp black peppercorns
1 large bunch coriander, with
  roots
2 tbsp dark sesame oil
3 tbsp fish sauce
8 spring onions, thinly sliced
500g cooked egg noodles
sliced chillies, to taste
  (optional)

You can now buy Chinese-style ready-roasted ducks in many supermarkets – alternatively, ask your local Chinese restaurant for a roast duck.

Remove the legs and breasts from the duck, and cut into portions, then either slice or shred the meat, whichever you prefer.

Chop the duck carcass into four or five pieces and put them in a pot. Cover with about 4 litres of water and bring to the boil. Skim any fat from the surface, then turn the heat down to a simmer and add the carrots, celery, onion, leek, ginger, star anise and peppercorns. Simmer for 1 to 2 hours, or until the stock has reduced by half, skimming the surface regularly.

Meanwhile, pick the leaves from the coriander and set aside. Wash, dry and chop the stems and roots, and reserve them separately.

When the stock has reduced, strain it through a fine sieve into a clean saucepan. Bring back to the boil then reduce the heat to a simmer. Add the sesame oil and fish sauce. Crush the coriander stems and roots, add them to the soup and simmer for a further 20 minutes.

Just before serving, add the spring onions, noodles and chillies (if using). Divide the duck and noodles between serving bowls, then pour the soup over the top. Scatter with coriander leaves and serve immediately.

Little dishes, little plates of deliciousness that surprise with huge flavours, that have no real rule as to when they should be eaten or how they should be eaten – these are the things that follow in this chapter.

Has the world of eating changed, or is it just my own personal preference to eat dishes from virtually anywhere in the world all at the same time? For me not being restricted to one cuisine is exciting and makes a meal far more enjoyable. Small dishes, bits and pieces that get plonked on the table or handed around are the way forward when it comes to impressing not just your friends but your taste buds.

I have always loved the vibrancy of Asia and many of the dishes here have been influenced by my travels in Thailand and styles of cooking that have stayed with me from growing up in Australia, where Indonesia and Thailand are our neighbours. I have also included a true childhood favourite, one that I still hold in high regard: the great chicken and stuffing sandwich. Brilliant in its simplicity, and brilliant for being both comforting in winter and satisfying in summer – even when packed for a picnic and the added crunch of sand has somehow made it into the mix.

snacks & starters

SPRING ROLLS WITH CHICKEN AND PRAWNS

MAKES

50g vermicelli noodles
2 garlic cloves
1 coriander root
5 white peppercorns
1 pinch salt
1 tbsp vegetable oil, plus 1.5
    litres for deep-frying
50g prawn meat, minced
50g minced chicken
2 tbsp fish sauce
1 tbsp palm sugar
100g beansprouts, topped and
    tailed
2 tbsp coriander leaves
2 tbsp sliced Chinese shallots
15 spring roll wrappers
4 tbsp plain flour
sweet chilli sauce, to serve

Spring roll wrappers can be found in packs of 50 in the freezer section of Chinese supermarkets. Divide the ones you don't need for this recipe into two batches, wrap them in cling film and pop them back in the freezer for another day.

Soak the noodles in warm water for at least 10 minutes, then drain and cut into 2cm pieces with scissors. Meanwhile, pound together the garlic, coriander root, peppercorns and salt in a mortar until fine, or blend in a food processor.

In a wok, heat 1 tablespoon of oil over a medium heat and fry the garlic paste until fragrant. Add the minced prawns and chicken, and fry until cooked, about 3 minutes. Add the noodles, then the fish sauce and palm sugar. Transfer the mixture to a bowl and allow to cool.

Mix the beansprouts, coriander leaves and shallots into the cooled mince mixture. Lay the spring roll wrappers on a board, a few at a time, and place 1 tablespoon of the filling along the centre of each wrapper.

Roll up the bottom edge of a wrapper and then fold over the left and right sides. Roll the wrapper until it has almost reached the top edge. Mix the flour with 2 tablespoons of water and use this paste to seal the roll. Repeat with the rest of the ingredients.

Heat the oil for deep-frying to 220°C. Working in batches of six or so, deep-fry the spring rolls for about 3 minutes, turning them over towards the end of cooking so that they are coloured all over. Drain and let the spring rolls cool a little before serving with the sweet chilli sauce.

CHICKEN IN PANDAN LEAF

MAKES

800g chicken meat with skin, minced
4 tsp Thai oyster sauce
1 tbsp black bean sauce
1 spring onion, chopped
2 garlic cloves, sliced and deep-fried
12 pandan leaves
vegetable oil, for deep-frying

Chicken in pandan is mainly cooked on the street rather than in restaurants and is usually made with cubes of chicken soaked in red vinegar and soy. A Thai lady showed me this recipe using chicken mince. The pandan leaves impart a smoky flavour when deep-fried, but don't try to eat them.

In a bowl, mix together all the ingredients except the pandan leaves and oil for deep-frying. Divide the chicken mixture into twelve balls.

Clean and flatten the pandan leaves. Hold one leaf with the pointed end to the sky. Place a chicken ball 4cm from the base then fold the end of the leaf up over the chicken. Twist the remaining leaf around the chicken so as to cover all the meat. Push the pointed tip under the first layer and pull tight to secure the parcel.

Heat the oil for deep-frying in a wok or deep-fryer. Grasp the pandan leaves in a bunch, holding them by the pointed end, and when the oil is hot enough to deep fry, gently lower the parcels into the oil. Fry for 7 to 8 minutes or until cooked through and serve immediately.

SALT AND PEPPER
LEMON CHICKEN

SERVES

1 litre vegetable oil
10 white peppercorns
20g sea salt
100g plain flour
grated zest of 1 lemon
500g chicken thigh fillets, with
  skin
mayonnaise, soy sauce or
  sweet chilli sauce, for serving

Slowly heat the vegetable oil in a wok or deep-fryer. Meanwhile, pound the peppercorns and sea salt together in a mortar then stir in the flour and lemon zest. Heat the oven to 180°C (gas 4) and put a baking tray in it to heat at the same time.

When the oil starts to shimmer it is ready for cooking. Toss the chicken in the seasoned flour until well coated. Drop a quarter of it in the oil and fry for about 4 or 5 minutes. When the chicken is done it should float to the top of the oil, curl and turn crisp.

Remove the chicken from the oil and place on the hot baking tray in the oven while you fry the remainder in batches. Serve with little bowls of mayonnaise, soy sauce or sweet chilli sauce.

PORTUGUESE CHICKEN CROQUETTES

MAKES

2 chicken breasts, about
   200g each
50g butter
1 tbsp chopped onion
3 tbsp plain flour, plus extra
   for coating
225ml milk
150g sliced ham, chopped
1 tbsp English mustard powder
1 tbsp chopped parsley
2 eggs, beaten
200g dry breadcrumbs, for
   coating
1 litre vegetable oil
salt and pepper

Be careful with these, they are wonderfully addictive and once you have started eating them someone may come home and find you in the corner surrounded by crumbs. They stay hot for a good 10 minutes so make brilliant little party snacks. You could also make them with turkey.

Poach the chicken in enough salted water to cover for 10 minutes and leave to cool in the liquid (you can also use chicken left over from your Sunday roast). Once cool, put the cooked chicken in a food processor and blend to smooth paste.

Heat the butter in a saucepan and fry the onion. Add the flour to make a paste and cook, stirring constantly, until it begins to brown. Gradually add the milk and continue cooking and stirring for 10 minutes. Stir in the chicken, ham, mustard and parsley. Add some salt and pepper and mix well. Let the mixture cool a little to form a thick paste.

Shape the mixture into croquettes the size of small sausages. Dust all over with flour, dip in the beaten eggs, then coat with the breadcrumbs, pressing them on really well. Put the croquettes on a tray in the fridge to set for a good hour.

When ready to cook, heat the oil in a wok or small deep-fryer. When it starts to shimmer, drop in a few croquettes and fry until they are golden and float to the top of the oil – they should take 4 or 5 minutes. Drain the cooked croquettes on paper towel while you cook the rest in batches.

Let the croquettes cool a little before serving because if you bite into them straight away they will burn your bloody mouth, mate.

ROAST CHICKEN AND STUFFING SANDWICH

SERVES

butter and lots of it
2 big thick slices white bread
mayonnaise
cold or hot roast chicken,
   stripped from the bone
cold, or maybe even hot,
   stuffing
1 handful rocket

Butter the bread, spreading one of the slices with lots of mayonnaise too. Pile the chicken on, and the stuffing. Add some rocket. Cover with the other slice of bread and squish down before cutting in half.

Also good with: watercress 🐓 pea tops 🐓 coleslaw 🐓 little gem 🐓 iceberg

GRILLED CHICKEN WITH GUACAMOLE

SERVES 🐓🐓🐓🐓🐓🐓🐓🐓🐔🐔

6 chicken breast fillets
olive oil
corn chips, to serve
salt and pepper

GUACAMOLE
200 plum tomatoes, cubed
1 small red onion, diced
8 basil leaves
1 large handful parsley, leaves
  picked
1 long red chilli, finely diced
30ml olive oil
½ tsp Tabasco sauce
2 limes, halved
2 avocados
1 large bunch coriander

Grill the chicken breasts following the method on page 62 and set aside.

To make the guacamole, put the tomatoes and onion in a mixing bowl. Roughly chop the basil and parsley leaves and add to the bowl along with a good pinch of salt and a grind of pepper. Add the chilli, olive oil, Tabasco and a good squeeze of lime. Leave to one side – it will hold for a few hours if need be.

Peel the avocados, remove the stones and cut the flesh into hunks. Place in a bowl and squeeze the juice from one of the limes over it. Drain off 2 tablespoons of the juice that has come out of the tomatoes and add to the avocado. Mix with a fork until it becomes a chunky mash, then chop half the coriander and add it along with the tomato-onion mixture.

Slice, shred or pull the chicken and serve it with the guacamole. Garnish with the rest of the coriander. You might want to put a big squeezy bottle of mayo and some cold beers on the table too.

DEVILLED CHICKEN LIVER CROSTINI

MAKES

10 chicken livers, cleaned and fat removed

4 sage leaves, fresh or preserved in salt, plus 16 fresh sage leaves to garnish (optional)

4 juniper berries

4 tbsp olive oil

1 garlic clove, peeled but left whole

125ml dry red wine

16 pieces Tuscan bread, about 7.5cm square and 5mm thick

salt and pepper

Heat the oven to 200°C (gas 6). Finely chop five of the chicken livers together with four sage leaves and the juniper on a board.

Heat the oil in a small heavy saucepan over a medium heat. Add the chopped ingredients and the garlic and sauté for 10 minutes. Pour in the wine and let it bubble away for 10 minutes.

Put the bread on a baking sheet and heat in the oven for 10 minutes. Meanwhile cut the remaining chicken livers into quarters and add them to the saucepan. Season with a bit of salt and pepper and cook for 4 minutes. Remove the pan from the heat and transfer the contents to a crockery or glass bowl.

To make the canapés, spread a tablespoon of the topping over each piece of bread. Arrange the crostini on a large serving platter and, if fresh sage is available, place one leaf on top of each to garnish.

BREADED CHICKEN LIVERS WITH BÉARNAISE

SERVES 🐔🐔🐔🐔🐔🐔

100g plain flour
2 eggs
a little milk
200g fine dry breadcrumbs
24 chicken livers
400ml vegetable oil
salt and pepper

BÉARNAISE SAUCE
100ml white wine vinegar
1 shallot, chopped
a few sprigs of tarragon
2 egg yolks
120g warm melted butter

What is important is that these little morsels are cooked fairly slowly so that the meat is pink at the centre but the crumbs stay beautifully golden and crisp.

Put the flour in a bowl and season well with salt and pepper. Beat the eggs and milk together in a bowl and set it next to the flour. Line up the breadcrumbs in a third bowl. Working one or two at a time, roll the livers in the flour, then dip them in the egg and lift out, letting the excess egg drain off. Finally, roll the livers in the breadcrumbs, patting them on firmly and making sure they are thoroughly coated. Set aside.

To make the sauce, put the vinegar, shallot and tarragon in a saucepan and boil until the mixture has reduced by about three-quarters. Let it cool, then pour it into a large stainless steel bowl. Set the bowl over a pan of barely simmering water. Add the egg yolks and whisk until you can see the whisk leaving a pattern in the sauce. Remove the bowl from the heat and start to add the melted butter, little by little, whisking all the time until all the butter is used. Season to taste and set aside.

Heat the oven to 150°C (gas 2). Put a large heavy frying pan over a medium heat with 200ml of the oil. Once hot, lay six to eight livers in the pan – they should sizzle a little. Cook for a good minute on each side until golden but not dark brown – reduce or raise the heat to get the desired effect. Put the cooked livers on a baking tray in the oven to keep warm while you fry the remainder. Serve hot with the béarnaise sauce.

CHOPPED LIVER AND ONIONS

SERVES

100g schmaltz, ground
300g chicken livers
300g onions, finely diced
3 hard-boiled eggs, peeled and chopped
1 handful chopped parsley
rye bread and gherkins, to serve
salt and pepper

The important part here is the schmaltz – that is the chicken fat from inside the cavity of the raw bird, which is very good indeed. If you don't have any use a little vegetable oil.

Heat the schmaltz in a frying pan until it melts. Add the livers and onions and cook for a good 15 minutes, stirring constantly. Season with lots of salt and pepper as it cooks. Remove from the heat and cool for 5 minutes.

Tip the contents of the pan onto a chopping board and, with a big knife in each hand, chop the mixture like mad as though you were mincing it. About halfway through, add the eggs and continue chopping until the mixture is almost a paste.

Serve with some chopped parsley, rye bread and gherkins.

CHINESE CRISPY
DUCK PANCAKES

SERVES

1 large Chinese roast duck
  (page 174)
20 Chinese pancakes
sliced cucumber
sliced spring onions
hoi sin sauce

If your duck is cold, reheat it at 220°C (gas 7) for 40 minutes. Meanwhile, steam the Chinese pancakes over hot water and get your other accompaniments ready on separate plates.

Take the duck from the oven and shred the meat with two forks. Serve with the pancakes, cucumber, spring onions and hoi sin sauce, for guests to compile and wrap themselves at the table.

AUBERGINE AND
MISO PICKLE

SERVES

vegetable oil, for deep-frying
3 large aubergines
180g red miso
120g sugar
120ml chicken stock (page 20)
4 spring onions, cut at an angle
10g togarashi or chilli powder

DRESSING
120ml light soy sauce
45g sugar
135ml rice vinegar
30ml sake
1-2 red chillies, finely diced
45ml groundnut oil

Another great way to serve Chinese roast duck.

Heat the oil in a deep-fat fryer to 220°C. Meanwhile, cut the aubergines into 2cm cubes. When the oil is hot, fry the aubergine until brown then drain on paper towels.

In a saucepan, heat the miso, sugar and stock for a few minutes. Add the fried aubergine and cook until soft. Add the spring onions and chilli powder, and remove from the heat.

To make the dressing, combine the soy sauce, sugar, vinegar, sake and chillies in a small bowl and blend in the oil. Serve the pickle with your Chinese roast duck on top and some of the dressing spooned over.

GRILLED QUAILS WITH SPICED LENTILS

SERVES

LENTILS

100ml olive oil, plus extra
  virgin olive oil for drizzling
2 red onions, finely chopped
1 leek, finely chopped
1 carrot, finely chopped
3 garlic cloves, crushed
1 handful thyme leaves
a few sage leaves, chopped
400g puy lentils
5 tomatoes
3 spring onions, chopped
a dash of red wine vinegar
1 handful coriander
1 handful flat-leaf parsley,
  chopped

BOUQUET GARNI

1 carrot, halved lengthwise
1 leek
1 sage sprig
3 thyme sprigs
1 celery stick, halved
  lengthwise

QUAIL

16 boned quails (page 59)
a little olive oil
salt and pepper

Quail is a sweeter meat than chicken. The birds are small, but the eating is easy if the bones are taken out, and licking your fingers at some stage is mandatory.

Start with the lentils. Heat the olive oil in a heavy pan and gently sweat the onions, leek, carrot, garlic, thyme and sage until the vegetables are just soft. Add the lentils.

Make the bouquet garni by tying the carrot, leek, sage, thyme and celery in a bundle with kitchen string and add it to the pot of lentils. Add enough water to cover the lentils, plus a little more, then cook the lentils at a gentle simmer for about 30 minutes (don't boil the love out of them, as the Italians say!).

Add the tomatoes and continue simmering very gently for about 30 minutes or until the lentils are soft but still have a slight bite to them. You will need to top up the water every now and then: the finished lentils should have a slightly soupy consistency.

Meanwhile, if you haven't already done so, bone the quails following the method overleaf.

Heat a griddle. Season the birds and rub with oil. When the griddle is hot, place the quail on it skin-side down and cook for 2 minutes, then turn them over and do the same. Repeat so the total cooking time is 8 minutes, and the meat will be perfect.

Finish the lentils while the quail is cooking. Add the spring onions, season well and cook for another 10 minutes. Pour in the vinegar. Fold in the coriander and serve with parsley and extra virgin oil.

SALT AND PEPPER QUAIL WITH SWEET CHILLI SAUCE

SERVES 🐓 🐓 🐓 🐓 🐓 🐓

1 litre vegetable oil
10 white peppercorns
20g sea salt
100g plain flour
10g garlic cloves
6 boned quails (see opposite)
1 large handful coriander, picked

CHILLI DRESSING

3 dried chillies, roasted and deseeded
50g palm sugar
juice of 2 limes
125ml fish sauce

To make the dressing, pound the roasted dried chilli in a mortar then add the palm sugar and pound again, adding the lime juice and fish sauce. Mix well and set aside.

Heat the oven to 180°C (gas 4) and put a baking tray in it to heat up at the same time. Meanwhile, slowly heat the vegetable oil in a wok or deep-fryer. Pound the peppercorns and sea salt together in a mortar, then add the flour and set aside.

Peel half the garlic and pound it with the remaining whole cloves – the cloves should split open and the flesh and skin should come together. Throw the pounded garlic into the hot oil, lower the heat to a bubble and leave to cook for a good 5 minutes, stirring every so often. When done, the garlic will float to the top and be crisp. Lift out the garlic with a strainer and drain well on paper towel.

Reheat the oil: when it starts to shimmer it is ready. Toss the quails in the seasoned flour so that they are well coated. Drop three quails in the oil and fry for about 4 or 5 minutes, or until they turn crisp. Remove from the oil and place on the hot tray in the oven while you cook the remainder.

Put the fried garlic and picked coriander in a large bowl and add a smidgen of the chilli dressing. Toss well and serve on individual plates with the quails propped on top and the dressing around the outside.

CRISP FRIED QUAIL
AND GREEN MUSTARD

SERVES 🐔🐔🐔🐔🐔🐔🐔🐔🐔🐔

½ bunch spring onions, finely diced

50ml soy sauce, plus extra to garnish

10 boned quails (see below)

2 litres vegetable oil, plus 50ml for stir-frying

100g potato flour

20g Chinese five-spice powder

20g ginger, peeled and cut into julienne

500g green mustard leaves, split lengthways

25g yellow bean paste

50ml oyster sauce

The day before serving, combine the spring onions and soy sauce in a big bowl. Add the quails and marinate for 24 hours if possible.

Heat the oil in a deep-fat fryer to 220°C. Mix together the potato flour and five-spice powder. Remove the quails from the marinade and pat on the flour mixture without draining them too much. Working in batches of three or four, place the quails in the hot oil and fry for about 4 minutes. Drain on paper towels and keep in a warm oven while you deep-fry the rest.

Heat a wok with 50ml of vegetable oil. Add the ginger then the green mustard leaves and yellow bean paste, and cook, stirring, for about 3 minutes. Remove from the heat and add the oyster sauce. Cover the wok and leave the greens to braise in its warmth for about 10 minutes.

You can serve the quail and greens on individual plates with dabs of soy sauce around the sides, but I like to pile them up on a large platter in the middle of the table and let people help themselves.

HOW TO BONE QUAIL

Use scissors to cut down each side of each quail's backbone and lift it out. Hold the bird in both hands and push the breast with your thumbs, applying pressure to the rib cage and the breast-plate. Turn the splayed bird on to a board, skin-side down, so you can see the bones and ease them away with your fingers. Use a small knife to take out the thighbone by slipping the knife under the bone and cutting it out.

Ah, that age-old question: legs or breasts? It still divides the world, but I reckon there is always time for the breast and there is always time for the leg. The difference is quite simple – one is soft and sweet but needs time and nurturing (the leg), the other is lean and mean and quick to cook (the breast) but needs accompaniment from something else to really bring it to life, to stimulate and bring out its beauty.

Grilling a breast has become a favourite regular supper for many. The bitter exterior of the skin should be crisp and the flesh soft and moist, but it needs a worthy partner to set it up as a trophy plate. You can do what you want as a side, from the classic chips and mayo combination to more sophisticated and spicy dishes like harissa and stewed chickpeas. Fill it with garlic butter and protect its delicate flesh and boom! You've got the great chicken kiev. And when done well, it is the great kiev.

The leg – ah, now that is my true friend. Love legs, but they need time and for that the old ones are the best. Schnitzels or southern fried – either way is great by me, thanks.

legs & breasts

GRILLING CHICKEN

Most chicken that has been grilled has been cooked to death. It's
dry and nasty and no longer tastes of the beautiful chook. Heat is
the secret – not too much of it – and the skin must stay on to
protect that soft, white flesh. The chicken will be cooked through
properly if you just let it go slowly. Cook it too fast and the outer
will be dry and the inside still raw – and what a turn-off that is.

I realise most people prefer chicken breasts, but for me the
flavour of the meat and skin on the legs and thighs is far, far
better. You can cook them just as easily if you buy leg and thigh
joints that have been boned out. Don't try to grill them with the
bones still in – the result will be tough.

Heat a griddle until hot then turn the heat down. Season the
chicken with salt and just a little bit of pepper, and rub oil all
over it. Gently lay the chicken skin-side down on the griddle and
leave it to sizzle for 4 or 5 minutes so that it cooks nice and
slowly. Turn it over and give it just a few minutes on the other
side, then turn it back on to the skin side and repeat the process,
adding a good knob of butter and some more salt.

The rules for barbecuing chicken breasts and legs are a bit
different from those for grilling. The fat from the skin can cause
flare-ups on the barbie so do not rub oil all over, just on the flesh
side. Place the chicken skin-side down over the hot coals and
cook for 5 minutes, then put the barbecue cover on and cook for a
further 3 minutes. Turn the breast or thigh over, place some
butter (or flavoured butter) on top so it melts into the skin and
put the cover back over the barbecue. Leave to cook for 3 more
minutes. Check to see that the barbecue isn't too hot (no flames
here please) and, if necessary, take the cover off. Then leave the
chicken to cook for another 5 minutes or so. Take the chicken
from the heat and keep it warm, then slice and serve.

CHIPS & MAYO

Fry the chips in three batches so the oil reheats quickly and browns the chips nicely.

6 large potatoes, peeled and cut into 3cm chips
5 litres corn or vegetable oil
salt
120ml mayonnaise
4 lemon wedges
4 handfuls watercress

Soak the chips in cold water for 5 minutes, then change the water and leave to soak for another 5 minutes. Meanwhile, heat the oil to 140°C in a deep-fat fryer. Drain the chips and pat them dry with paper towel.

Fry each batch of chips for 8 to 10 minutes, then drain well and leave on a tray to cool. Afterwards, heat the oil to 190°C and, still working in batches, fry the chips for 2 minutes. Give them a little shake, then cook for another 4 to 5 minutes until well-coloured. Drain the chips for a few minutes before sprinkling them with salt and serving with the chicken, mayo, lemon and watercress. SERVES 4.

PANZANELLA

This salad is best after a bit of rough and tumble (not you, the salad). It needs to be worked together so all the flavours blend.

100ml red or white wine vinegar
a big bowl of leftover bread, cut into
    thumb-sized chunks
6 ripe tomatoes, roughly chopped
1 red onion, chopped
1 large handful chopped flat-leaf parsley
chopped olives and peppers (optional)
50g pine nuts, toasted
about 3 tbsp John's vinaigrette (page 101)

Mix the vinegar and 100ml water in a jug, pour over the bread and stir so the bread soaks up the flavour. Squeeze the bread to get rid of the excess liquid and set aside.

Put the tomatoes in a large bowl, giving half of them a squeeze. Add the onion and parsley, stir, then add the bread and mix well. Add the rest of the ingredients and stir again. Leave for a good 20 minutes while you cook the chicken. SERVES 6.

GINGER CHICKPEAS & HARISSA

50ml vegetable oil
2 tsp garam masala
120g fresh ginger, peeled and finely chopped
1 red chilli, deseeded and finely chopped
400g can chickpeas, drained
400g can chopped tomatoes
1 large handful coriander leaves, coarsely
    chopped
4 heaped tbsp harissa
lemon wedges or halves, to serve
salt and pepper

Heat the oil in a saucepan until smoking. Add the garam masala and sizzle for 30 seconds, then add the ginger and chilli and stir well. Add the chickpeas, stir again to coat them in the spices, then add the tomatoes, a good pinch of salt and a good grind of pepper. Bring to the boil, then remove from the heat and stir in the coriander.

Serve with the chicken, lemon and a dollop of harissa on the side. SERVES 4.

POMEGRANATE, SPINACH & OLIVE SALAD

The crisp, bittersweet skin of the chicken, the crunchy pomegranates and olives, and iron-rich spinach combine beautifully in this simple salad.

1 whole pomegranate
24 large green olives, sliced
juice of 1 lemon
2 tbsp olive oil
2 handfuls spinach leaves
salt and pepper

Scoop the seeds from the pomegranate and mix them in a bowl with the sliced olives, lemon juice and olive oil and leave them to sit for 20 minutes while you cook the chicken. Shred the spinach and season it with salt and pepper.

To serve, chop or slice the cooked chicken, put it on serving plates and scatter the salad ingredients over the top. SERVES 4.

THAI CUCUMBER SALAD

50g palm sugar
50ml fish sauce
200ml coconut milk
1/2 cucumber, halved and deseeded
2 small shallots (the little Thai ones, if possible),
   sliced very thinly
1/2 small red pepper, deseeded and cut into thin strips
2 long red chillies, deseeded and cut into thin strips
1 large handful coriander leaves
4 lime leaves, torn (optional)
1 handful Thai basil leaves
100g roasted peanuts, chopped

Combine the palm sugar, fish sauce and coconut milk
in a heavy frying pan, bring to the boil, then simmer for
a good 10 minutes. Set aside to cool.
   Use a vegetable peeler to cut the cucumber into long,
thin strips and put them in a bowl with the shallots,
pepper and chillies. Pour the cooled dressing over the
veg and leave to stand for 10 to 15 minutes. Stir in the
herbs and sprinkle the nuts over the top. SERVES 6.

SALSA VERDE & MASH

Traditionally served with boiled meats, salsa verde
(green sauce) is delicious with chicken as well as pork
and fish. Make it in advance of serving if you wish – it
will hold for few days in the fridge. Serve the chicken
and sauce with mashed potato, following my recipe on
page 157.

1 handful flat-leaf parsley
1 handful basil
2 garlic cloves, peeled and crushed
1 boiled egg
1 handful fresh white breadcrumbs
1 tbsp white wine vinegar
1 tbsp capers, drained
50ml olive oil
1 pinch salt

Put the parsley, basil and crushed garlic in a food
processor and blend to a paste. Add all the remaining
ingredients and blend for 2 minutes. SERVES 4.

SEA-SPICED AUBERGINE

2 medium aubergines, cut into 1cm strips
125ml vegetable oil
2.5cm ginger, peeled and cut into matchsticks
4 spring onions, thinly sliced at an angle
3 red chillies, deseeded and thinly sliced
4 tbsp oyster sauce
1 tbsp fish sauce
2 tbsp coriander leaves

Put the aubergine strips in a wok, cover with cold water
and bring to the boil. Drain the aubergine and allow it
to cool, then pat it dry.
   Dry the wok and place it over a high heat. Add the oil,
then the ginger and aubergine. Cook for 5 to 6 minutes
until the aubergine is evenly browned (avoid stirring
too much as this will make it mushy). Stir in the chillies
and three-quarters of the spring onions. Drain off most
of the oil, then return the wok to the heat. Stir in the
oyster and fish sauces and cook for a final 2 minutes
before adding the remaining spring onions and
coriander. SERVES 4.

HOUMOUS & PAPRIKA

400g freshly boiled chickpeas, still in their water
3 tbsp tahini
4 garlic cloves
juice of 4 lemons
100ml olive oil, plus extra for serving
salt and white pepper
paprika, for sprinkling

While the chickpeas are still hot, drain and reserve the
cooking water. Put the chickpeas, tahini and garlic in a
food processor and blend to a paste. Add half the lemon
juice, half the oil and a teaspoon of salt. Blend and, as
it starts to thicken, add a little of the cooking water and
then some more lemon juice and olive oil.
   Keep adding all three until the houmous is like a thick
sauce (it will thicken as it cools). Adjust the seasoning,
adding more lemon if you want a kick and more oil for
a peppery flavour.
   To serve, swirl the houmous over the plates, add the
grilled chicken, sprinkle with paprika and drizzle with
olive oil. SERVES 4.

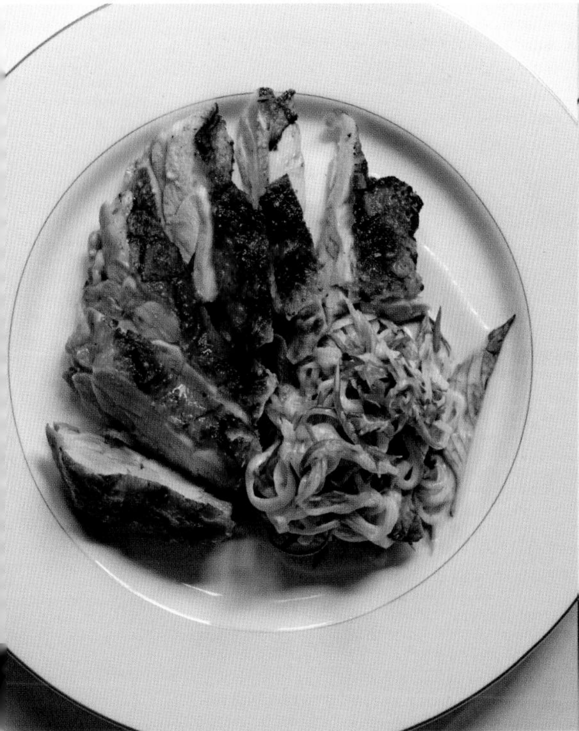

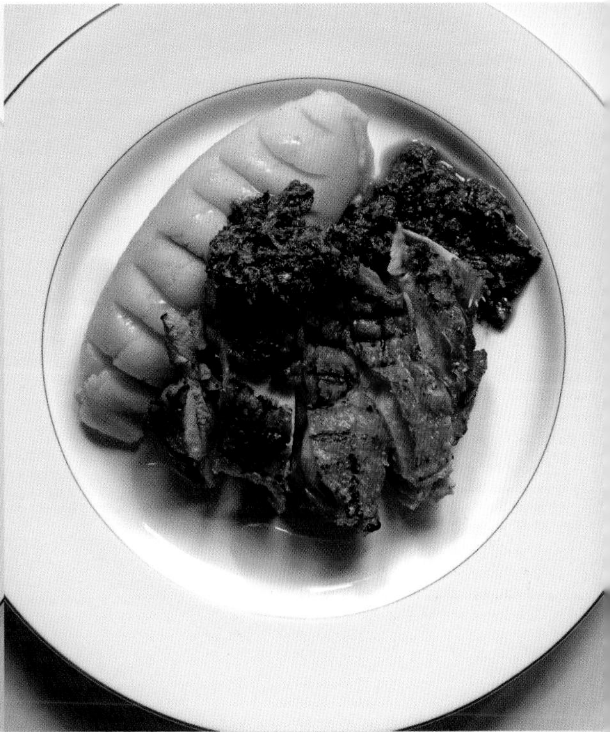

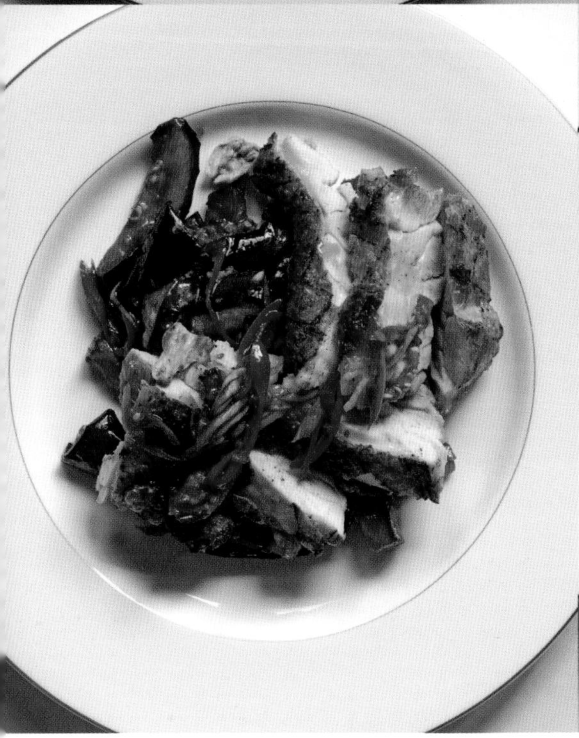

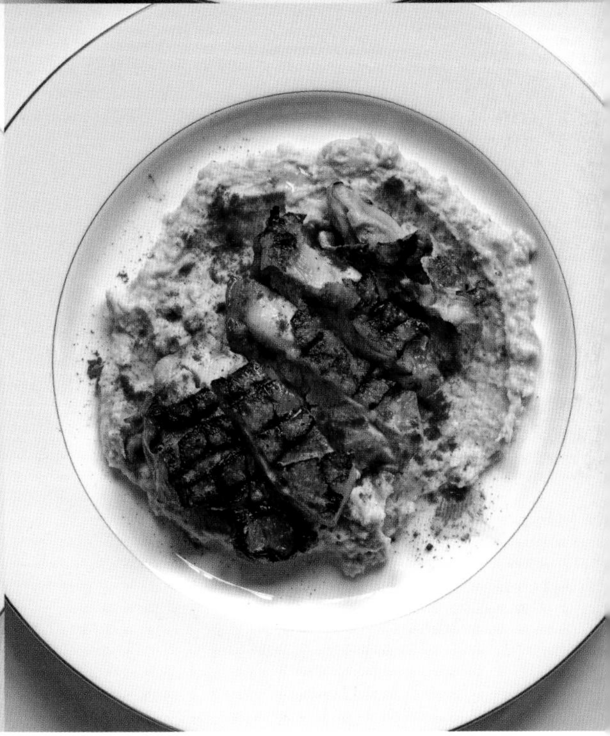

CHICKEN KIEV

SERVES

50g butter, softened
1-2 fat cloves garlic, finely
  chopped
2 tbsp chopped fresh parsley
1/2 tsp finely grated lemon zest
2 tsp lemon juice
2 skinless chicken suprêmes
  (breast with wing bone left
  on)
3-4 tbsp plain flour
1 tsp paprika
1 large egg
100g dried breadcrumbs
sunflower oil, for frying
flaky sea salt and pepper

TO SERVE
mashed potatoes (page 157)
wilted spinach

Who could not love chicken kiev? Soft, sweet delicious chicken crusted with crisp breadcrumbs, and herb-rich butter flowing from the centre – that, my friend, is the perfect chicken kiev and this is the perfect recipe.

To make the filling, mix together the butter, garlic, parsley, lemon zest and juice, and some salt and pepper. Shape into two logs and chill until firm but not solid.

Heat the oven to 190°C (gas 5). Make a slit lengthwise in each chicken breast and open out like a book. Lay each flat between two pieces of cling film with the bone pointing away from you and bash with a meat mallet or rolling pin until 5 to 10mm thick. Place a log of butter on each flattened breast 2cm in from the edge then roll up the chicken and secure with cocktail sticks.

Mix the flour, paprika and some salt and pepper together in a shallow bowl. Beat the egg in another shallow bowl. Toss the stuffed chicken breasts in the flour until coated and shake off any excess. Slide the chicken into the beaten egg and turn until covered, then cover each chicken breast with flour and egg once more. Finally, dip the chicken into the breadcrumbs and turn to coat completely, again shaking off any excess.

Pour oil into a medium frying pan to a depth of about 1cm and heat thoroughly. Toss in a small cube of bread to check the temperature – it should sizzle and brown straight away. Lower the chicken breasts carefully into the pan and spoon some of the hot oil over the top for about 1 minute to seal the crumbs. Turn over to brown the other side, again spooning oil over the top until the crust is golden – this should take a further 1 or 2 minutes.

Transfer the chicken to a shallow roasting pan and bake uncovered for 12 to 14 minutes, or until the breasts feel firm when pressed. Remove and drain on paper towel. Carefully remove the cocktail sticks and serve with mashed potato and spinach.

CHICKEN WITH TARRAGON SAUCE

SERVES

olive oil
2 chicken breasts, skin on
salt and pepper

TARRAGON SAUCE
100ml brandy
100ml crème fraîche
1 handful chopped parsley
1 handful torn tarragon leaves

Although we've put this with mash in the picture, it's just as nice with champ, or chips.

Heat a heavy frying pan over a medium heat and add a little olive oil. Season the chicken well and place it skin-side down in the pan. Cook for a good 8 minutes, then turn the breasts over and cook for the same time again. Check the chicken is cooked through, then remove it from the pan and keep warm.

Raise the heat under the pan to very high. Add the brandy and carefully flame it to burn off the harsh taste of alcohol. Shake or stir to incorporate the pan juices and sticky bits from the base of the pan. Stir in the crème fraîche then taste and season. Bring the sauce to the boil and reduce by half. Add most of the parsley and tarragon leaves.

Serve the sauce with the chicken and some mash or champ, pouring the brown juices that come from the rested chicken over the dish as well. Sprinkle with the last of the chopped herbs.

SOUTHERN FRIED CHICKEN

SERVES

1 whole chicken, cut into 8
  pieces
1¹/₂ tsp salt
1.5 litres vegetable oil, for
  frying
200g plain flour
1 tsp ground white pepper
2 tsp cayenne pepper
2 tsp paprika
2 tsp allspice
2 tsp ground thyme
2 eggs, beaten

TO SERVE
gravy (page 156)
lemon wedges
mayonnaise

**Give this a whirl and you will never buy takeaway
again. Well, you might, but it won't be as good as this!**

Score the skin of the chicken pieces then place them in a large
bowl of cold water with a good teaspoon of salt and leave to soak
for 2 hours.

Mix together all the dry ingredients, including the remaining
¹/₂ teaspoon of salt, and set to one side. Take the chicken from
the water and pat it dry with paper towels. Drop the chicken into
the flour mixture and toss to coat each piece well. Set aside for
10 to 15 minutes.

In a deep-fryer, heat the oil ready to cook the chicken, and please
be very careful. At the same time, heat the oven to 180°C (gas 4).
Sit a wire rack inside a roasting tin and put them in the oven to
heat as well.

Coat the chicken pieces in the beaten egg and drop them in the
seasoned flour again. When the oil has reached 220°C, put two or
three pieces in the oil, cook for a good 6 to 8 minutes then
remove them to a tray. Bring the oil back to the correct
temperature and repeat the frying until all the pieces are cooked.

Transfer all the fried chicken to the wire rack in the hot oven and
bake for a further 20 minutes until cooked through. Cut open a
piece to check they are done: the chicken should not be pink near
the bone. Serve hot with some gravy, wedges of lemon and mayo.

TURKEY ESCALOPE CORDON BLEU

SERVES

4 thin slices turkey breast,
    about 225g each
4 slices ham from the bone
4 slices emmental cheese
vegetable oil, for frying

GARLIC HERB BUTTER
3-4 tbsp chopped flat-leaf
    parsley
3-4 tbsp chopped chives
1 tsp chopped tarragon
115g unsalted butter, softened
2 garlic cloves
1/2 tsp English mustard powder
salt and pepper

CRUMB COATING
50g plain flour
2 eggs, beaten
175g fresh breadcrumbs

An oldie but a goodie.

Start with the garlic herb butter. Put the herbs and softened butter in a bowl. Crush the garlic cloves together with a little salt until you have a smooth paste then add to the butter mixture. Add the mustard and some pepper, and mix well. Divide the butter into four little logs, wrap in cling film and chill to harden.

Put each piece of turkey between two sheets of cling film and bash with a mallet or rolling pin until they are very thin and about the size of a small plate. Lay the breast fillets on a board, smooth side down, and season with pepper. Lay a slice of ham and then a slice of cheese over each. Unwrap the flavoured butter, place a piece in the middle of each turkey-ham-cheese combo and fold up like an envelope.

Line up the flour, beaten eggs and breadcrumbs in three separate shallow dishes. Dip each turkey parcel into the flour, making sure it is well coated. Continue, dipping the parcels into the eggs, then the crumbs, making sure at each stage that they are well coated. Put the parcels on a tray and chill for 30 minutes before cooking.

Heat the oven to 180°C (gas 4). When ready to cook, heat the oil in a large frying pan. Add the turkey parcels and cook for 2 minutes on each side. Transfer the parcels to the hot oven to continue cooking for about 5 minutes, or until golden. Remove the turkey parcels from the oven and drain on paper towels before serving.

SCHNITZELS

SERVES

4 skinless chicken thigh fillets, bashed out to about the size of your hand
100g plain flour
2 eggs, beaten with a little milk
200g fine dry breadcrumbs
vegetable oil, for frying
salt and pepper

It is important that these are cooked fairly quickly so that the meat is cooked in the centre but the crumbs stay beautifully golden and crisp. (Yes they have to be crisp – no soggy schnitzels thanks). You could serve them straight up with lemon and cornichons, or in a big floury bap with lettuce, tomato or beetroot, and mayonnaise.

Heat the oven to 150°C (gas 2). Put the flour in a bowl and season well with salt and pepper. Put the bowl of beaten egg mixture next in line, and a bowl of breadcrumbs last. Roll the chicken fillets in the flour, then dip into the egg, letting the excess drain back into the bowl as you lift them out. Next, roll the chicken in the breadcrumbs, patting them down firmly and making sure they are well coated all over. (You may find it easiest to coat all the chicken in the flour, then all in the egg, then all in the crumbs.)

Put a wide, heavy frying pan on the stove and get it hot. Add 2 tablespoons of oil and once the oil is hot, slide in two schnitzels (assuming they fit of course, I am hoping that your pan is big enough to get a couple of these things in it, if not more). They should sizzle a little. Cook for a good 4 minutes on each side until they are golden (not dark) brown: lower or increase the heat to get the desired effect.

Transfer the schnitzels to the oven to stay warm while you cook the remainder, adding more oil if the pan is a bit dry, but let it get hot before you add the schnitzels.

DUCK BREASTS

There is a great secret to cooking the perfect duck breast with a crisp skin, moist flesh and pink centre and that secret is a cold frying pan and no oil. It's true.

Take four duck breasts; don't trim them. Lay them flesh-side down on a board and use your knife to score the skin all the way through to the flesh – but so that the blade just touches the flesh, do not cut into it. Make sure you score all the way to the edge of the breast so that as the skin shrinks during cooking it doesn't pull the flesh in and make it tough. Season the skin (only the skin side) with a generous amount of salt and ground black pepper.

Take a solid, heavy frying pan and turn the heat to three quarters on your stove to get it going. Lay the duck skin-side down in the cold pan and then put the pan over the heat and turn the heat down to about half. Now do not touch anything, do not move the pan – I said don't touch, don't even think about it. What is going to happen over the next 10 minutes is the fat under the skin will slowly melt and the skin will go brown and crispy.

When the skin starts to colour around the outside you are ready to move on. The pan should have a good 1 to 2cm of duck fat in it and all the fat from the breast should have melted. Season the flesh side now and not before, then turn the duck breasts over, cook for 2 minutes and increase the temperature to full, for just 1 more minute. Take the pan from the heat and leave the breasts in the pan for 5 minutes while you finish off your side dishes, then slice and it will be very sexy indeed.

You can keep the rendered duck fat for cooking roast potatoes simply by draining it into a heatproof glass bowl and storing it in the fridge. Four duck breasts will produce around 200ml of duck fat. If you get some brown jelly at the bottom of the bowl, don't worry – that's just concentrated duck stock and will keep fine as long as it is covered by the duck fat.

ROAST PUMPKIN AND PINE NUTS

2kg piece pumpkin, or 1 butternut squash, peeled
  and deseeded
40ml olive oil
a little fresh oregano
50g pine kernels, toasted
2 tbsp John's vinaigrette (page 101)
lemons halves or wedges, for serving
flaky sea salt and pepper

Heat the oven to 200°C (gas 6). Cut the pumpkin or
squash into 3cm chunks and toss with the oil and
seasoning in a roasting tray. Cook for 50 minutes on the
top shelf of the oven, until tender.

Mix the pumpkin, oregano and pine kernels in a large
bowl and spoon over the dressing. Mix well but gently
and serve with the duck and lemon. SERVES 4.

BOK CHOY AND CHILLI

2 tbsp vegetable oil
2 garlic cloves, chopped
6 heads bok choy, halved lengthwise
50ml oyster sauce
20ml light soy sauce
1 red chilli, finely sliced

Heat the oil in a wok. Add the garlic, fry for 2 minutes,
then add the bok choy and stir-fry for 2 minutes or until
it wilts. Pour in the oyster and soy sauces, along with
50ml of water. Cook for a further minute then sprinkle
with the chilli, toss and serve with the duck. SERVES 6.

COURGETTE FRITTERS

200g plain flour
2 tsp baking powder
1 large pinch salt
1 tsp paprika
3 eggs
100ml milk
2 large courgettes, grated
olive oil, for frying
a little soured cream (optional)
mustard, for serving
salt and pepper

Sift the flour, baking powder, salt and paprika into a
large bowl, then make a well in the centre. In a separate
bowl, whisk together the eggs and milk. Add the egg
mixture to the dry ingredients and whisk until you have
a smooth, stiff batter. Mix in the grated courgettes.

Heat a little oil in a non-stick frying pan then drop in
a good ladle of batter per fritter and cook until golden
brown on both sides. Sprinkle the cooked fritters with a
little olive oil, some salt and black pepper, and some
soured cream if you like, before serving with the duck
breasts and a spoonful of mustard. SERVES 4.

CELERIAC MASH

275g celeriac, peeled and cubed
125ml milk
125ml olive oil, plus extra for drizzling
125ml water mixed with a little lemon juice
25g parsley
salt and pepper

Put the celeriac in a saucepan with the milk, olive oil
and enough water to cover. Season then bring to the
boil and cook uncovered for about 20 minutes over a
low heat. Test the celeriac with a fork to make sure it is
soft, then strain and reserve the cooking liquid.
Roughly mash the celeriac with a fork. Mix in the
parsley and a little of the cooking liquid to give a soft
consistency and serve with the duck and a drizzle of
olive oil. SERVES 2.

WILD MUSHROOMS AND NEW POTATOES

500g jersey royal potatoes, or other new potatoes
2 tsp olive oil
2 garlic cloves
1 fennel bulb, cut into eighths
2 bay leaves
2 thyme sprigs
200g mixed wild mushrooms, cleaned
some dried morels
100ml white wine
salt and pepper

Par-boil the potatoes for 10 minutes, then drain and peel when cool.

Heat the oven to 180°C (gas 4). Heat the oil in a casserole. Add the garlic and a grind of black pepper, then the potatoes, fennel, bay leaves and thyme and stir. Cook for 4 minutes or until just starting to colour.

Add the mushrooms and dried morels and cook for 10 minutes over a high heat, stirring occasionally. Add the white wine, bring to the boil for 30 seconds, then cover and continue cooking for about 2 minutes.

Transfer the casserole to the hot oven for 15 minutes. When done, season well and serve hot with the duck. SERVES 6.

SKORDALIA

400g potatoes, peeled and cubed
5 garlic cloves
100ml milk
100ml olive oil, plus extra for drizzling
juice of 1 lemon, plus lemon halves or wedges
   for serving
salt and white pepper

Put the potatoes in a heavy saucepan with the garlic, milk, olive oil and some seasoning and place over a medium heat. Bring to the boil and cook for 15 to 20 minutes until the potatoes are soft.

Remove from the heat and strain off and reserve the cooking liquid. Blend the potatoes in a food processor with the lemon juice and half the cooking liquid, then return the skordalia to the saucepan and reheat. Serve with a drizzle of olive oil alongside the duck and with lemon halves or wedges on the side. SERVES 2.

CRUSHED PEAS AND MINT

600g frozen peas
1 handful mint, stalks and leaves separated
3 spring onions, chopped
50g salted butter
100ml double cream
olive oil, for drizzling (optional)
lemons halves or wedges, for serving

Put the frozen peas in a medium saucepan with the mint stalks, pour over 100ml of boiling water from the kettle and place over a high heat. Add the spring onions and butter, bring to the boil and cook for 3 minutes. Add the double cream and return the peas to the boil.

Remove the pan from the heat and, using a food processor, blend the pea mixture for a minute or so. Chop the mint leaves and add them to the pea purée as you gently reheat it. Spoon a good amount onto each serving plate, top with the cooked duck and maybe a drizzle of olive oil and serve with lemon. SERVES 4.

OLIVES AND BUTTON ONIONS

The idea of gigantic salty olives with sweet button onions, a hint of chilli and a good splash of sherry vinegar to get the digestion of that rich duck going is, for me, a real beauty.

10g butter
100g button onions, peeled
200g large purple and green olives, pips removed
   and flesh squashed
1/2 tsp dried chilli flakes
30ml sherry vinegar

Melt the butter in a heavy saucepan. Add the onions, turn the heat down low and cook slowly for 10 minutes – don't let them go brown. Add the olives and chilli flakes and give a good stir. Increase the heat a bit and cook for 5 minutes. Add the vinegar and turn the heat right up. Let it boil and that's it: serve with the duck. SERVES 4.

PIGEON WITH BACON
AND SWEETCORN FRITTERS

SERVES 🐔 🐔 🐔 🐔 🐔 🐔

3 pigeons
olive oil
12 rashers streaky bacon
about 100ml soured cream
salt and pepper

SWEETCORN FRITTERS
200g plain flour
2 tsp baking powder
1 tsp paprika
3 eggs
100ml milk
200g can sweetcorn, drained
2 spring onions, sliced
1 handful chopped coriander
1 handful chopped parsley

To make the sweetcorn fritters, sift the flour, baking powder, paprika and a good pinch of salt into a large bowl. Make a well in the centre. In a separate bowl, combine the eggs and milk. Gradually add the egg mixture to the dry ingredients and whisk until you have a smooth, stiff batter. Add the sweetcorn, spring onions and herbs and set aside.

Heat the oven to 180°C (gas 4). Rub the pigeon with oil and season well with salt and pepper. Place a heavy frying pan over a medium heat and, when the pan is hot, add 1 or 2 tablespoons of oil. Lay the pigeons on their side in the frying pan. Let them colour well then turn to the next side and repeat, then turn and colour again. Pop them in the oven. After 3 minutes give the pan a little shuffle and cook for a few minutes more – the birds should be very pink.

Heat a little oil in a non-stick frying pan and, working two or three at a time as necessary, cook six fritters, frying them until golden brown on each side. As the fritters cook, put them on a baking tray and keep warm in the oven. At this stage I would turn the oven to very low. While the fritters are cooking, fry the bacon in a separate pan and keep it warm in the oven too.

Carve the breasts from the pigeons. To assemble the dish, place a corn fritter on each serving plate and top with two rashers of bacon and a pigeon breast. Spoon some soured cream over the top and sprinkle with a little olive oil and some salt and pepper.

PHEASANT WITH CABBAGE ROLLS

SERVES

4 pheasant
olive oil
salt and black pepper

SAUCE
25g butter
125g shallots, chopped
50g garlic cloves, chopped
50g mushrooms, sliced
100ml sherry vinegar
200ml dry sherry
500ml chicken or game stock
(page 20-21), plus about
300ml extra

CABBAGE ROLLS
1 savoy cabbage
100g veal or pork mince
2 large shallots, chopped
50g cooked white rice
1 handful chopped parsley

Start the sauce. Melt half the butter in a small saucepan and sweat the shallots, garlic and mushrooms until soft and golden. Deglaze the pan with sherry vinegar, letting it reduce to a syrupy consistency. Add the dry sherry and when it is very hot carefully flame the pan. Keep boiling until the volume of liquid has reduced by half, then add the stock and reduce on a lower heat, skimming often. When the sauce is a light jus, season to taste then pass through a fine sieve and set aside.

Meanwhile, make the cabbage rolls. Strip away the cabbage's outer leaves until you have eight good ones. Finely slice the rest of the cabbage. Bring a pot of salted water to the boil and blanch the sliced cabbage for 1 minute. Refresh under cold water and drain well. Next blanch and refresh the big cabbage leaves and leave them to drain on a kitchen cloth. Remove the central vein if it is fibrous and thick.

Heat the oven to 180°C (gas 4). In a large mixing bowl, work the sliced cabbage, mince, shallots, rice, parsley, and some salt and pepper together with your hands until completely mixed. Place an egg-sized pile of filling on each cabbage leaf. Fold in the ends and roll into a cigar making sure no filling can escape. Put the cabbage rolls in an ovenproof dish and pour in enough stock to come three-quarters of the way up the sides of the rolls. Braise in the oven for 30 to 40 minutes.

Meanwhile, heat a large ovenproof frying pan on the stovetop. Rub the pheasants with oil and seasoning and cook, turning, until well coloured. Transfer to the oven and roast for 15 minutes. Allow them to cool slightly before carving.

Return the sauce to the pan and reduce it further. Just before serving whisk in the remaining butter. The sauce should have a delicate sweet and sour taste and be barely a coating consistency. To serve, place a breast and leg on each plate together with two of the cabbage rolls and coat with 2 or 3 tablespoons of the sauce.

It must be fresh, it must be balanced. It needs bits of crisp and crunchy, it needs bits of soft and succulent. It needs the acid of an unctuous dressing and the sweetness and fragrance of soft herbs.

The meat for your salad – be it poached, grilled, or cold leftovers from a roast – is best torn or shredded. A good salad is really fork food, relaxed food, not something that you should work over while you eat. You do all the work in the composition: the chopping and poaching, the roasting and slicing, mixing the dressing or cooking the sauce – all done, all organised, all cooled and all ready to plop in a bowl. A handful of this and a handful of that and then a delicate stir.

Whether you like your salad served in a big bowl or as a single pretty little plate, it don't matter, just take the time to organise and get all those bits ready so the first time you stick your fingers in the bowl and find it needs a bit more of something, it is there ready.

Otherwise, there are no rules in this chapter. Many of the dressing recipes make more than you need for one salad. I believe that if something lasts you should make plenty of it and use the rest over the next few days – bugger the washing up.

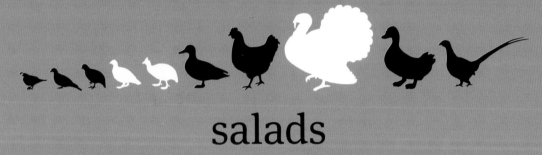

salads

HOW TO POACH A CHICKEN

1 carrot
1 onion
1 leek
1 celery stick
1 chicken, about 1.15kg
2 bay leaves
1 small bunch parsley
$^{1}/_{2}$ tsp black peppercorns

I usually use roast chicken for salads but if you prefer poached chicken, here's how to do it perfectly.

Cut the vegetables into biggish pieces and put in a pot with the chicken, bay leaves, parsley, peppercorns and just enough water to cover. Poach gently for 40 minutes then remove from the heat and allow the bird to cool in the liquid.

Once cool, lift the chicken from the pot and use as desired. Strain the stock and use it for other dishes.

CHICKEN, CRAB AND AVOCADO SALAD

SERVES

200g plum tomatoes, deseeded
and cubed
1 small red onion, finely diced
8 basil leaves, roughly
chopped
2 tbsp roughly chopped
parsley leaves
1 tbsp olive oil
1/2 tsp Tabasco sauce
1 tbsp balsamic vinegar
200g roast or poached chicken,
cooled and shredded
200g fresh white crabmeat
2 avocados
4 lemons, halved
1 handful coriander sprigs
salt and pepper

The sweetness of the crab and the tomatoes goes well with the shredded roast chicken, punchy dressing and rich avocado.

Put the tomatoes, onion, basil and parsley in a mixing bowl with a good pinch of salt and a grind of pepper. Add the olive oil, Tabasco and balsamic vinegar, and set aside.

Mix the chicken with the crabmeat and set aside (it will hold for a few hours if need be).

Peel the avocados and remove the stones. Mash the flesh with a fork then squeeze over the juice from one of the lemons. Drain off 2 tablespoons of dressing from the tomatoes and add it to the avocado.

To serve, place a few large spoonfuls of tomato salad on a plate, top with some of the chicken and crabmeat, then the avocado. Scatter with the coriander and sit the lemon halves on the side.

CHICKEN WITH COCONUT DRESSING

SERVES 🐓🐓🐓🐓🐓🐓

50g palm sugar
50ml fish sauce
400g can coconut milk
6 chicken thigh fillets
2 red Thai shallots
½ red pepper, cut into julienne
2 small red chillies, cut into
  julienne
50g cucumber, cut into
  julienne
10g roasted peanuts
4 lime leaves, cut into very fine
  julienne
30 coriander leaves
6 squares banana leaf, to serve

Bring the palm sugar, fish sauce and coconut milk to the boil in a large saucepan, add the chicken and poach until the chicken is cooked through. Leave to cool.

Mix the other ingredients (except the banana leaves) together in a bowl. When the chicken is cool, cut it into 1cm thick strips and toss into the salad.

Lay a banana leaf at the centre of each plate and pile on the salad. Drizzle with some of the poaching liquid and serve.

CHICKEN LARP

SERVES

400g finely minced chicken
30ml fish sauce
90ml lime juice
8 red Thai shallots, sliced
4 tbsp mint leaves
4 tbsp coriander leaves, plus
    coriander sprigs to garnish
4 tbsp roasted rice powder
    (page 98)
1 tbsp chilli powder, toasted
finely shredded chillies
salt

This seriously fiery dish burns your mouth like you wouldn't believe but I love it. Reduce the quantity of chilli powder and shredded fresh chillies if you like.

Simmer the chicken in a pan with a little salted water for 3 minutes or until cooked, stirring often. Remove from the heat and cool to room temperature.

Just before serving add the fish sauce, lime juice, shallots, mint and coriander leaves, roasted rice and chilli powder. Check that flavour is hot, salty and sour. If necessary, add a few extra drops of lime juice to sharpen and define the flavour. Serve sprinkled with the shredded chillies and extra coriander.

CHICKEN CAESAR SALAD

SERVES

100ml vegetable oil

100g pancetta, cut into lardons

2 thick slices white bread, or
½ baguette

200g parmesan cheese, grated,
plus 60g parmesan cheese,
shaved

4 little gem lettuces, leaves
separated, or 1 large cos
lettuce, leaves torn into large
pieces

60g anchovy fillets, cut in half
lengthwise

4 large chicken breasts, grilled
and sliced (page 62)

pepper

DRESSING

1 medium egg plus 1 egg yolk

1 tbsp Dijon mustard

1 tbsp shallot vinegar

2 anchovy fillets, finely
chopped

1 garlic clove, crushed

200ml vegetable oil

200ml olive oil

There is something about freshly washed crisp lettuce, still slightly wet and very well chilled, covered in creamy dressing. Anchovies should be included but if you don't want them that is fine, just add a little salt. You will have more dressing than needed but it will keep in the fridge for a few days. Do bear in mind that it contains raw egg.

In a heavy frying pan heat the vegetable oil, add the pancetta lardons and fry gently over a medium heat moving constantly so they don't stick or burn.

When crisp, remove from the pan with a slotted spoon and drain on kitchen paper.

Cut the bread into 1cm cubes and add to the oil in which the pancetta was cooked. Fry for a few minutes until well coloured on all sides, then remove with a slotted spoon and drain on kitchen paper. While the croutons are still warm, place in a bowl and sprinkle over 1 to 2 tablespoons of the grated parmesan.

To make the dressing, whisk the egg, egg yolk, mustard, vinegar, anchovies and garlic in a large bowl until the mixture begins to thicken and turn pale. Slowly add the oils, whisking constantly, until well amalgamated. Add a little hot water if the mixture seems too thick. Stir in the rest of the grated parmesan.

To serve, place the lettuce leaves in a bowl and toss with enough of the dressing to coat thoroughly. Scatter with the croutons, pancetta, chicken and anchovy fillets, and finish with the shaved parmesan and a grinding of black pepper.

SMOKED CHICKEN COB SALAD AMERICAN DINER STYLE

SERVES

200g cooked, peeled beetroot
50g redcurrant jelly
20ml red wine vinegar
6 palm hearts, halved
    lengthways or sliced
2 cos lettuces, leaves separated
200g can sweetcorn, rinsed
    and drained
3 rashers cooked bacon, diced
200g crumbly blue cheese such
    as stilton
400g smoked chicken, thinly
    sliced
4 hard-boiled eggs, quartered
50ml Caesar dressing (page 94)
flaky sea salt and pepper

Cut the beetroot in quarters and place in a saucepan over a high heat with the redcurrant jelly and vinegar. Bring to the boil and cook for 10 minutes or until the beets are well coated and the sauce sticky. Set aside to cool.

Divide the palm hearts and lettuce between eight serving plates. Arrange the beetroot on top of the leaves and sprinkle with the sweetcorn and bacon bits. Crumble the blue cheese roughly into 2cm pieces and place on top. Add the sliced smoked chicken, then a couple of egg quarters per plate. It will look a bit messy but that is the idea. Sprinkle over some salt and pepper and drizzle with Caesar dressing before serving.

CORONATION CHICKEN CUPS

MAKES

2 roast or poached chickens, cooled
3 tbsp good-quality curry powder, or the equivalent in paste
500ml mayonnaise
200ml double cream
100g raisins
4 little gem lettuces
1 handful picked chervil, to garnish

Strip the chickens of their meat and discard all cartilage and skin. Tear the meat into small finger-sized pieces and put in a large bowl.

In another bowl, mix the curry powder or paste with the mayonnaise, then stir in the cream and raisins. Pour the dressing over the chicken and fold together well, but be careful not to over-mix as the cream could split.

Trim the bases of the little gem and pick away the leaves until you have enough to give 24 good-sized lettuce cups. Arrange them on a large platter and spoon some of the chicken mixture into each one. Garnish with the chervil and they're ready to serve. To eat, you pick up the lettuce cups, wrap the lettuce around the filling and bite.

SPICED DUCK SALAD, THAI HERBS AND ROASTED RICE

SERVES 🐔🐔🐔🐔🐔🐔🐔🐔

DUCK
4 duck legs
3 tbsp fish sauce
10cm galangal, bashed
3 lemongrass stalks, bashed
11 lime leaves
100ml coconut milk

SALAD
100g Thai fragrant rice
2 green papaya, or 4 Thai
   green mangoes, peeled and
   cut into julienne
25g snake beans or string
   beans, finely chopped
25g Chinese cabbage, thinly
   sliced
4 long red (serrano) chillies,
   deseeded and finely chopped
1 bunch Thai basil

DRESSING
1 red Thai chilli
1 green Thai chilli
2 tbsp fish sauce
2 tbsp lime juice
1 tbsp palm sugar
1 tbsp caster sugar
1 tbsp tamarind water
   (page 114)

You only need a little roasted rice to add crunch to this recipe, but it is worth roasting a jar full and keeping it to pop into any salad. I prefer to cut the papaya in strips rather than pound it, as is traditional in Thailand.

The day before serving, rub the duck all over with the fish sauce and leave, skin side down, in this marinade for 12 hours or so.

Next day, heat the oven to 220°C (gas 7). To make the roasted rice, put the rice in a bowl, cover with water and leave for 5 minutes before draining. Scatter the rice over a baking sheet and roast for about 30 minutes, until the grains turn off-white, begin to pop and develop a nutty fragrance. Transfer to a bowl to cool, then grind the roasted rice to a powder and store in a jar.

To cook the duck, shake off the excess fish sauce and place the legs in an ovenproof dish with the galangal, lemongrass and three of the lime leaves. Pour the coconut milk over the top and cook in the oven for about 2 hours. Turn the oven down to 180°C (gas 4) and continue baking for another hour, until the duck meat falls away from the bone easily.

Remove the duck from the oven. Lift off the skin and lay it on a rack in a roasting pan. Return it to the oven for about 30 minutes, until the skin is dry and crisp. Crumble and reserve.

In a large bowl, combine the papaya, beans, cabbage, chillies, basil, a handful of roasted rice and the remaining lime leaves, which should be cut into thin strips. Shred the duck meat and add it to the bowl.

At the last minute, combine all the dressing ingredients, pour over the salad and toss to coat. Serve immediately, before the vegetables start to go limp.

DUCK WITH POMELO, WATERMELON AND CASHEWS

SERVES

4 duck legs, cooked and
   shredded as on page 98
½ daikon radish
1 pomelo
200g watermelon, cut into
   chunks
100g cashews
3 spring onions, cut into strips
1 carrot, shredded
1 large handful coriander,
   picked
1 large handful Thai basil,
   picked
4 little gem lettuces
20 chives, for tying

DRESSING
1 red Thai chilli
1 green Thai chilli
2 tbsp palm sugar
2 tbsp fish sauce
2 tbsp lime juice
1 tbsp tamarind water
   (page 114)

If you have not already done so, cook the duck legs and shred the meat.

To make the dressing, crush the chillies in a mortar, add the palm sugar and pound to a paste. Stir in the fish sauce, lime juice and tamarind water and continue to pound until the dressing is well mixed. Set aside.

Use a mandoline grater or a vegetable peeler to shred the daikon into thin strips approximately 6cm long and 2mm thick. Peel the pomelo then take the segments between your fingers and rub them so that the flesh breaks into small pieces.

In a mixing bowl combine the daikon, pomelo, watermelon, cashews, spring onions, carrot, coriander and basil.

Refresh the lettuces in cold water to make them crisp. Remove the two outer leaves and discard, then peel the leaves away one at a time until you get to the hearts. Shred the hearts of the little gem and add them to the salad bowl along with the duck meat. Stir the dressing into the salad and leave to sit for 2 minutes so the vegetables wilt slightly.

Take the remaining lettuce leaves and place a good spoonful of salad in the centre of each one. Bring in both ends and then roll up to make a parcel. Tie with the chives and serve immediately. Alternatively, put everything out on the table and let guests roll their own.

GOOSE, APPLE AND WATERCRESS SALAD

SERVES

2 granny smith apples
300g roast goose, cooled and
  thinly sliced
100g watercress, large stalks
  removed
1 handful flat-leaf parsley,
  picked
1 large handful toasted
  walnuts

JOHN'S VINAIGRETTE
  (MAKES 400ML)
1 tbsp dijon mustard
75ml red wine vinegar
1 tsp walnut oil
300ml olive oil
flaky sea salt and pepper

This works a treat: sour apples, peppery watercress and a simple but punchy vinaigrette. It is very simple to make and perfect for leftover goose, which is sometimes a difficult meat to use up.

To make the dressing, whisk the mustard and vinegar in a bowl until blended. Slowly add the oils, still whisking, and season to taste. The dressing will keep for up to 1 month in an airtight jar in the refrigerator.

Peel and core the granny smiths and slice them into thin wedges, about twelve to an apple. Place them in a large bowl with all the remaining salad ingredients and mix well. Drizzle with some of the dressing and serve, with extra dressing on the side for those who want it.

WOOD PIGEON, PLUMS AND COBNUTS

SERVES

4 plums
1 tbsp sugar
1 glug brandy
12 black peppercorns
2-3 thyme sprigs, leaves picked
4 wood pigeons
100ml olive oil, plus extra for
    rubbing
1 tbsp vegetable oil
12 cobnuts
2 handfuls mixed leaves,
    sprouts and cress
juice of 1 lemon
salt and pepper

This little salad is quick and very delicious. Cobnuts are simply hazelnuts. 'Cob' is an old English word for head and a hazelnut is shaped like a bald head. The best come from Kent and are available fresh in late autumn – otherwise use hazelnuts, which can be bought in bags all year round.

Stew the plums in a little water with the sugar and brandy for 20 minutes, then cool and slice thinly.

Meanwhile, heat the oven to 180°C (gas 4). Grind the whole peppercorns until fine and mix with 1 teaspoon of salt and the thyme leaves. Rub the pigeons lightly with olive oil, then rub the pepper mixture over the inside and the outside of the birds.

Heat a large ovenproof frying pan until very hot. Add the vegetable oil and sear the pigeons on all sides. Transfer the pan with the birds to the oven. At the same time, spread the nuts on a baking tray and put them in the oven to toast. Both the nuts and birds will need 6 to 7 minutes.

Take everything from the oven and leave to cool. Cut the breasts from the carcasses and slice them thickly.

Put the cobnuts, plums and greens in a mixing bowl and pour over the oil and lemon. Give a good grind of black pepper and a liberal sprinkle of salt. Mix well. Pile on plates, top with the pigeon and eat – yes, go on, that's it, delicious.

PIGEON SALAD WITH PANCETTA AND BEANS

SERVES

200g green beans, topped and
tailed
100g pancetta lardons
4 wood pigeons
100g canned flageolet beans,
rinsed and drained
3 endive, quartered

DRESSING
100ml extra virgin olive oil
2 tbsp shallot vinegar
2 tsp strongly flavoured jus or
stock
2 tbsp diced shallots
salt and pepper

Bring a saucepan of salted water to the boil. Drop in the green beans and when they return to the boil, cook for 1 minute before draining and refreshing them under cold water. Set aside.

Heat the oven to 200°C (gas 6). Whisk all the ingredients for the dressing in a bain-marie over steaming water until the mixture has emulsified. Set aside to cool.

In an ovenproof frying pan, fry the pancetta until golden. Use a slotted spoon to remove it from the pan and drain on paper towel. Season the pigeons, then fry them in the bacon fat to give them some colour. Transfer to the oven and roast for 3 to 4 minutes, keeping them pink.

When the pigeons are done, drain off and reserve the pan juices. Strip the meat from the bones and cut the breast into thin strips.

In a large bowl, toss together the green beans, flageolet, bacon and a little of the dressing, adding some of the pan juices from the pigeon. Season well then add the pigeon meat and toss again.

Arrange three pieces of endive on each serving plate and pile on the salad. Finish with a little more of the dressing and some freshly ground pepper.

PARTRIDGE SALAD WITH ROAST PARSNIPS AND CHESTNUTS

SERVES

2 small parsnips, peeled and
sliced into discs
2 good-sized partridges
olive oil
1 big handful thyme sprigs
1 large shallot, diced
100g rocket and endive or
dandelion leaves
100g chestnuts, roasted and
chopped
1 big handful chopped parsley
John's vinaigrette (page 101)
salt and pepper

Drink a big, heavy red wine with this rich, homely autumn salad to celebrate the slippery slope into winter's gutsy foods after a summer of lettuce. It's best served at room temperature: hot food and salad leaves do not mix well, they just turn to silage.

Heat the oven to 170°C (gas 3). Plunge the parsnip slices into a pan of boiling water for 2 minutes, then drain and pat dry. Drizzle with some olive oil and set aside.

Rub the partridges with oil, season well with salt and pepper and fill the cavities with the thyme. Place a large ovenproof frying pan over a medium heat and, once hot, add 1 tablespoon oil and the birds. Cook, turning, until they are well coloured all over.

Add the parsnips to the frying pan and pop it in the oven. After 12 minutes give the pan a little shuffle and cook for a few minutes more, at which point the birds should be done.

Remove the partridges to a plate and put the frying pan over a medium heat. Add the diced shallot and let the pan juices boil dry so all the flavour goes into the veg, then set aside.

Toss the salad leaves together and, when the parsnips are cool add them and the chestnuts and parsley. Thinly slice the breast meat of the birds (keep the legs to make a pie, or something for the dog). Mix the partridge with the salad and drizzle with vinaigrette. Pile the salad on plates and serve with warm bread for lunch or as a starter.

PHEASANT SALAD WITH BEETROOT AND WATERCRESS

SERVES 🐦🐦🐦🐦🐦🐦🐦

2 pheasant
30ml olive oil, plus extra for
  rubbing
300g cooked, peeled beetroot
50g redcurrant jelly
20ml red wine vinegar
50ml Caesar dressing (page 94)
100g watercress
500g fresh, crumbly English
  goats' cheese
flaky sea salt and pepper

Beetroot has become trendy, let's rejoice. It is one of the most under-used vegetables in the patch. To be lazy (like I am) buy it ready-cooked and peeled in vacuum packs from the supermarket. If they're selling beetroot cooked in vinegar, all the better. I have to confess that I still eat the sliced stuff from cans. By the way, my father's favourite sandwich was sliced beetroot with peanut butter. Strange but true.

Heat the oven to 200°C (gas 6) and get an ovenproof frying pan hot on the stove top. Rub the pheasant with oil and seasoning and place in the hot pan. Cook, turning, until well coloured, then transfer to the oven and roast for 15 minutes. When done, leave to cool then shred the breast meat for the salad.

Meanwhile, cut the beetroot in quarters and place in a pan over a high heat with the redcurrant jelly and vinegar. Bring to the boil and cook for about 10 minutes, stirring until the beets are well coated and the sauce sticky. Set aside to cool.

When the beets are cold, mix them with the Caesar dressing and divide among six serving plates. Cover with a layer of watercress. If the goats' cheese has any rind, remove it, then crumble the cheese into pieces about 1cm square and scatter over the watercress. Add the pheasant meat and finally sprinkle the salads with salt, pepper and olive oil before serving.

CHICKEN LIVER SALAD

SERVES

12 chicken livers
1 tbsp redcurrant jelly
1 tsp cracked peppercorns
50g butter
20ml olive oil
1 splash wine vinegar
50ml madeira or marsala
1 tsp dijon mustard
100g mache lettuce
some other leaves, if you like
1 handful fresh redcurrants
salt

A simple and quick salad that is sweet from the booze and sour from the currants.

Heat a frying pan. Season the livers with salt and cracked pepper. Add the butter and oil to the pan then throw in the livers. Cook, tossing a few times until they get a decent colour – it should take no more than 5 minutes.

Add the vinegar and bring to the boil, letting it reduce by about half. Add the booze, boil again, then stir in the mustard and remove the pan from the heat.

Drain the sauce from the pan and mix a little of it with the leaves. Set up four plates and scatter the dressed leaves over them. Drop the redcurrants into the pan and toss. Divide the redcurrants and livers among the plates and drizzle with the remaining sauce.

You can make curry pastes easily in a food processor, however using a pestle and mortar really is best as they crush rather than rip the ingredients, resulting in a far better flavour. Using a pestle and mortar is also therapeutic, especially if you've got children.

I don't have a problem with you using bought curry pastes instead, but be aware that the preservatives used in them tend to give an acidic flavour. My recipes often include extra aromatics in the sauce to help counteract that.

The curry paste recipes in this chapter make more than you'll need for one dish, but it's not worth the trouble of making a smaller quantity. The excess keeps well in a glass jar in the fridge for 2 weeks. I like to divide mine into 2-tablespoon portions and store them in small plastic bags in the freezer, where they will keep for up to 6 months.

curries

THAI GREEN CHICKEN CURRY MY WAY

SERVES

2 x 400ml cans coconut milk
3 tbsp green curry paste (below)
800g skinless chicken thigh
   fillets, cut into three
6 lime leaves, shredded
3 lemongrass stalks, inner
   stalks only, chopped
20g galangal, sliced
1 tbsp palm sugar
1 tbsp fish sauce
1 handful pea aubergines
1 large handful beansprouts
1 large bunch Thai basil

GREEN CURRY PASTE
50g coriander seeds
25g cumin seeds
1 blade mace
1 tsp freshly grated nutmeg
9 garlic cloves, chopped
9 shallots, chopped
about 15 coriander stalks with
   roots, chopped, plus
   coriander leaves, to garnish
19 long green chillies,
   deseeded and chopped
250g galangal, chopped
5 lemongrass stalks, inner
   stalks only, chopped
2 tsp salt
5 lime leaves, stalks removed
   and leaves chopped
100g shrimp paste
1 handful Thai basil leaves

Don't let a green curry carry on cooking once the chicken is ready, otherwise the vibrant colour will begin to turn grey; it will also start to taste bitter rather than fresh and spicy-hot.

To make the curry paste, heat a frying pan (without oil), add the dry spices and roast until they begin to colour and release their aromas. Remove from the heat, let them cool a bit, then grind to a powder in a spice mill or blender.

Using a blender or a mortar and pestle, whizz or pound the garlic to break it down, then add the shallots and coriander roots and continue processing. Work in the chillies, galangal, lemongrass and salt. Finally, add the lime leaves, shrimp paste, basil and spice powder, and whizz or pound until you have a smooth paste. Set aside.

When making the curry, do not shake the cans of coconut milk. Instead, open them and scrape the fatty part of the coconut milk into a warm (not smoking) wok and cook it slowly, stirring all the time until it starts to bubble and sizzle and just begins to split. Add about 3 tablespoons of the green curry paste (you may need a bit more if it is a bought paste) and cook for a few moments until it releases its aroma.

Add the chicken, the rest of the coconut milk, the lime leaves, lemongrass, galangal, palm sugar and half the fish sauce. Let the sauce cook and bubble for about 15 minutes, until the oil in the coconut milk starts to come through to the surface.

Add the pea aubergines and the rest of the fish sauce and cook for a few minutes more. Stir in the beansprouts, scatter with the Thai basil and coriander leaves, and serve.

Tip: To make tamarind water, I tend to massage fresh tamarind paste in an equal volume of hot water until softened, then drain off the flavoured liquid.

MASSAMAN CHICKEN AND PRAWN CURRY

SERVES

100g coconut cream

100g massaman curry paste (below)

20ml fish sauce

20g palm sugar

60ml tamarind water

2 x 400ml cans coconut milk

1 pineapple, peeled, cored and cut into large pieces

10 lime leaves, torn

4 large red chillies, cut into pieces

2 lemongrass stalks, peeled and cut into 3cm pieces

6 skinless chicken thigh fillets, cut into 3 pieces each

about 20 large raw prawns, peeled and deveined

Thai basil leaves, to garnish

MASSAMAN CURRY PASTE

6 large red chillies, deseeded and chopped

2 lemongrass stalks, peeled and chopped

50g galangal, peeled and chopped

4 shallots, about 100g, sliced

6 garlic cloves, chopped

1 kaffir lime or 1 regular lime, chopped

20g ground white peppercorns

50g shrimp paste

20g roasted dried shrimps

This is a complex but beautiful Thai curry and, although time-consuming to make, it is also very satisfying. Unlike many Thai dishes you can serve it simply with some noodles or rice to give a whole meal. This recipe is for eight to ten people, but even if there are just four of you I bet you finish the whole bloomin' lot.

To make the curry paste, put all the ingredients in a food processor and blend until smooth. Taste and add some salt if necessary.

To make the curry, melt the coconut cream in a saucepan, stirring constantly to stop the cream burning. When it has separated, fry the curry paste in the fat until it is fragrant. Add the fish sauce, palm sugar, tamarind water and cook until the mixture darkens.

Add the coconut milk and pineapple and bring to the boil. Throw in the kaffir lime leaves, chillies and lemongrass, then add the chicken. Return to the boil and cook for 3 minutes. Add the prawns, bring back to the boil and cook for another 3 minutes.

Take the pan from the heat and leave it for 20 minutes to infuse while you cook your rice, or go for a fag, or a pint and a fag, or just a lager top. Return the curry to the stove, bring it to the boil and cook for 3 minutes. Serve garnished with some Thai basil leaves. Yum yum pig's bum.

CHICKEN DHANSAK

SERVES

LENTILS

250g red lentils

vegetable oil

1 garlic clove, crushed

2 large hunks root ginger, peeled, smashed then chopped

1 long red chilli, chopped

1 large onion, chopped

1 tsp cardamom pods, crushed

2 large ripe plum tomatoes, chopped

300ml chicken stock

1 handful coriander sprigs

50g butter

salt

DRY CURRY

2 tbsp coriander seeds

3 small dried red chillies

2 cloves

2 green cardamom pods

1 tsp cumin seeds

1 tsp fenugreek

1 tsp turmeric

1 tsp sea salt

100g ghee

3 large chicken or guinea fowl breast fillets, cubed

10 fresh or dried curry leaves

Here is an interesting curry – if you can really call it that. I'd say it is more like a great big lentil casserole with loads of wonderful smoky flavours of fenugreek and curry leaves. You can use guinea fowl in place of chicken if you like. This recipe easily serves up to eight people and will still give leftovers.

The day before cooking, leave the lentils to soak in cold water overnight. Next day, drain the lentils. Put them in a saucepan, cover with fresh water and add some salt. Bring to the boil and simmer until just tender. Remove from the heat and set aside.

Heat a little vegetable oil in a saucepan and fry the garlic, ginger, chilli and onion gently until golden. Add the cardamom and cook for a few seconds, then add the tomatoes and stock. Add the contents of the lentil pan and cook for a further 10 minutes.

Take out half the lentil mixture and purée it to a soup consistency. Stir this back into the remaining lentil mixture.

To make the dry chicken curry, toast all the spices, including the dried chillies, in a heavy-based pan for a good couple of minutes, until they are coloured and very fragrant. Leave to cool, then grind to a fine powder.

Melt the ghee in a wide, heavy-based pan and add the chicken (or guinea fowl) and curry leaves. Cook for a minute or so and give the bird a little colour. Add the ground spices and turn the heat down low while you mix the chicken and spices well. Raise the heat and cook for 2 to 3 minutes.

Pour in the lentil mixture, stirring well, then cover and reduce the heat again. Cook for 8 minutes then turn off the heat and leave to sit, covered, for 10 minutes. Stir in the butter, top with the coriander and serve with flatbread for scooping.

DRY CEYLONESE CURRY WITH TURKEY

SERVES

400ml can coconut milk
about 6 shallots, finely sliced
3 garlic cloves, finely chopped
1 thumb ginger, peeled and
  finely chopped
1-2 tsp chilli powder (choose
  how hot you want it to be)
¹/₂ tsp ground turmeric
1 stalk lemongrass, peeled and
  smashed
5cm piece pandan (screw pine)
  leaf (optional)
3-4 tbsp Ceylon curry powder
  (below)
500g turkey, guinea fowl or
  pheasant
juice of ¹/₂ lemon or lime
about 2 tbsp ghee

CEYLON CURRY POWDER
50g coriander seeds
30g cumin seeds
1 tsp fennel seeds
5cm cinnamon stick
¹/₂ tsp cloves
1 tsp green cardamom pods
³/₄ tsp fenugreek
10-12 curry leaves
1 tbsp raw rice

This is very similar to the Indonesian dish rendang, in which meat is boiled with coconut milk and spices. It is really more of a relish, with a marmalade-like sauce cloaking the meat. Serve with sticky rice or even little lettuce leaves for wrapping – it's a hot, sweet and sticky snack rather than a super-sized curry main course.

Do not use breast meat here as it will become too dry. Instead use something like turkey leg or thigh (pheasant and guinea fowl are other possibilities). Let it cook down really well: the meat will go through a few stages from tough to very tender and falling apart – this is where you want to be.

To make the curry powder, toast the spices and curry leaves in a hot, dry pan until fragrant (but do not let them burn or the curry will taste bitter). Remove from the pan and toast the rice separately. Leave to cool, then grind to a fine powder using either a spice mill or a mortar and pestle.

Shake the can of coconut milk well, then open it and pour into a saucepan or casserole. Add half the shallots and garlic, then stir in all the ginger, the chilli powder, turmeric, lemongrass, pandan leaf and three to four tablespoons of the Ceylon curry powder.

Pour in 200ml of water and bring the pan to the boil, mixing well as you add the poultry and lemon or lime juice. Simmer over a medium heat, stirring occasionally, for about 20 minutes or until the meat is cooked and the curry is thick.

Shortly before serving, heat the ghee in a frying pan or wok and fry the remaining shallots and garlic until aromatic and golden brown. Add this to the curry and stir well.

MALAYSIAN POTATO AND DUCK CURRY

SERVES

200g raw cashew or candle nuts
2 spring onions, finely chopped
vegetable oil
2 lemongrass stalks
40g ground coriander
1 tsp cumin seeds
1 tsp turmeric powder
100g block coconut cream
3 large shallots, finely chopped
6 garlic cloves, chopped
6 red chillies, deseeded and
  chopped
2 thumbs ginger, peeled and
  chopped
2 bay leaves
1-1.2kg duck leg and thigh
  meat, cut into 3cm cubes
2 x 400ml cans coconut milk
500ml chicken, vegetable or
  other stock, heated
20 new potatoes, peeled but
  kept whole

You can use duck breast here if you want to, but it tends to go a bit dry. Whatever pan you choose should be wide rather than deep because the liquid in the curry needs to boil away.

Bring a small pan of water to the boil and throw in the cashew or candle nuts. Turn off the heat and strain the nuts, then crush them to a paste in a mortar. Stir in the spring onions. Heat a little oil in a small pan and fry the nut paste until it is fragrant and lightly coloured, then set aside to use as a garnish.

Using a mortar and pestle, pound the lemongrass to a pulp, then remove from the mortar and set aside. In a frying pan, toast the coriander, cumin seeds and turmeric gently until fragrant, then grind to a fine powder in the mortar or using a spice mill.

In a wide pot or wok, heat the block of coconut cream until it melts, keeping the heat low so it does not burn. Drop in the shallots, garlic, chillies and ginger, and cook gently until the shallots have softened and the mixture smells beautifully fragrant. Add the toasted ground spices and the bay leaves, and fry for a few minutes more, until the mixture is really bursting.

Add the duck and increase the heat. Brown it well, stirring to coat it completely in the spices; it will take a few minutes. Add the coconut milk, bring to the boil then add the hot stock. Turn the heat up to high and continue cooking – the level of the liquid will quickly fall. After about 20 minutes, add the potatoes.

Reduce the temperature so that the sauce just bubbles and continue cooking very gently for 1 hour until the sauce is like lava and really coats the meat and spuds. Don't allow the mixture to simmer any harder or the spuds will break up. Finally, top the curry with the nut paste and serve.

MATT DAWSON'S
CREAMY TURKEY KORMA

SERVES

2 tbsp vegetable oil
500g turkey thigh meat, diced
1 red onion, thinly sliced
1 red pepper, chopped
1 courgette, sliced or chopped
2 garlic cloves, crushed
2 tbsp korma curry paste
½ tsp chilli paste, or chilli
  powder
230g can chopped tomatoes
150ml chicken stock
150ml double cream
50g creamed coconut, chopped
1 bunch coriander, chopped
salt and pepper

Rugby player Matt Dawson was the first celeb to take the 'Celebrity Masterchef' crown. He's a very good cook who understands what people like to eat and this (something he created for a celebrity recipe challenge promoting British turkeys) is what he likes to eat – delicious.

Heat the oil in a large saucepan and, working in batches, fry the diced turkey for 2 to 3 minutes or until lightly browned. Remove the turkey, allowing the excess oil to drain back into the pan, and set it aside.

Add the onion to the hot pan and fry for 5 minutes or until soft. Add the red pepper, courgette and garlic, and continue cooking for 5 minutes, stirring occasionally. Stir in the curry and chilli pastes, then add the tomatoes and stock, and bring to a simmer. Return the turkey to the pan and cook gently for 10 minutes.

Stir in the cream and coconut and cook for a further 1 or 2 minutes or until the coconut has melted and the sauce is bubbling. Season to taste and sprinkle with the coriander before serving with naan or rice and some mango chutney.

TURKEY AND SAAG ALOO

SERVES

2 tbsp ground coriander
2 tbsp ground cumin
2 tbsp ground turmeric
2 tsp salt
1 tsp mustard seeds
1 tsp chilli powder
4 garlic cloves, sliced
3 long red chillies, sliced
   (remove the seeds if you
   prefer)
100g ghee or clarified butter
2 large onions, diced
1 large potato, peeled and cut
   into cubes
500g skinless turkey breast
   meat, cut into thumb-sized
   chunks
200g large leaf spinach
2 tbsp yoghurt
1 small bunch coriander

I have always loved spinach and potatoes cooked with huge amounts of spice. This is something of a one-pot wonder, made with turkey, which is meant to be a good lean meat but I have fixed that with the addition of lots of butter. This is what food should taste like! You don't need a lot of food, though, so have more rice than curry. Enjoy.

Toast the dry spices in a hot pan for a minute or so, until they start to smell smoky. Transfer to a mortar with the garlic and two of the chillies and crush to a paste.

Heat the ghee or clarified butter in a heavy-based pan. Add the onions and fry until golden. Add the spice mix then turn the heat down. Add the potatoes and mix well. Keep frying for a few minutes, then pour in 100ml water, turn the heat up and bring to the boil. Cover and cook for 10 minutes, checking that the water does not evaporate completely.

Add the turkey and stir well, scraping the bottom of the pan to pick up any good bits. If the curry is dry, add a little more water. Cook for 5 minutes. Add the spinach and a little more water if the mixture seems to need it. Cook for 5 minutes, stirring constantly, then cover the pan, remove it from the heat and leave the spinach to steam for 2 minutes.

Take about 2 tablespoons of the spinach, combine it with half the yoghurt and purée this mixture in a blender. Stir the purée back into the curry and let it heat through for a moment. Transfer to a warmed serving dish and top with the rest of the yoghurt, sliced red chilli and fresh coriander.

JUNGLE CURRY OF GUINEA FOWL

SERVES

150ml vegetable oil

2 tbsp yellow curry paste (see below)

50ml fish sauce

1 guinea fowl, cut into 8 pieces

2 litres chicken stock or water

100ml Shaoxing wine

200g snake beans or green beans, cut into 7.5cm pieces

1 handful mangetout peas

200g bamboo shoots, cut into pieces

1 bunch Thai basil, leaves picked

100g karachi stalks or root ginger, scraped and cut into strips

30 lime leaves, torn

200g bok choy or choy sum, trimmed and divided into stalks

1 small bunch mint

YELLOW CURRY PASTE

30g dried shrimps

10g shrimp paste

3 garlic cloves, chopped

6 red shallots, chopped

50g galangal, chopped

19 long yellow chillies, deseeded and chopped

2 tsp salt

20g fresh turmeric

The jungle curry has its roots in the north of Thailand near the border with China. Coconuts do not grow in the north and so the area's traditional curries tend to contain more water and flavourings such as rich Chinese shaoxing wine. This sauce tastes deep and strong so holds up well against rich meats like guinea fowl or even pheasant and partridge.

First make the curry paste. Soak the dried shrimps in water for about 30 minutes, then drain. Meanwhile, wrap the shrimp paste in foil and toast it on a hot, dry pan until fragrant. Whizz the garlic and shallots in a blender (or pound in a mortar). Add the galangal, chillies and salt, followed by the shrimp paste, drained dried shrimps and turmeric. Blend to give a paste.

To make the curry, heat the oil in a wok or large saucepan and stir-fry 2 tablespoons of the curry paste for a few minutes, until it becomes fragrant. Add the fish sauce and continue frying for another minute. Add the guinea fowl pieces and cook with the paste for 5 minutes, so they get a little colour. Pour in the wine then the chicken stock or water, bring to a simmer and cook for 40 minutes.

Add the remaining ingredients and simmer for another minute, then turn off the heat. Cover and leave the curry to rest for 5 minutes to allow the flavours to infuse before serving.

PARTRIDGE IN CHILLI JAM

SERVES

3 partridges
100g pork fat or 120ml
   vegetable oil, plus extra oil
   for frying the birds
180g palm sugar
5 tsp fish sauce
200g gai lan or tenderstem
   broccoli
about 5 lime leaves, chopped
1 large handful Thai basil,
   chopped
deep-fried garlic and chilli
   slices, to garnish

CURRY PASTE
10g dried red chillies
30g dried red shrimps
9 large red serrano chillies,
   deseeded and chopped
1 red onion, chopped
17 garlic cloves
70g galangal, peeled and
   chopped
10g coriander roots, chopped
3 lemongrass stalks, peeled
   and chopped

First make the chilli paste. Snap the stalk end from the dried chillies and shake out and discard the seeds. Place the chillies in a bowl, cover with hot water and leave for about 30 minutes to plump up. Meanwhile, soak the dried shrimps in a bowl of cold water, also for 30 minutes or so.

Set up a steamer big enough to hold the birds and cook them over gently simmering water for 30 minutes. Remove from the heat, but leave the birds in the steamer.

Drain the hydrated chillies and shrimp. Put them in a blender with all the other ingredients for the curry paste and whizz to a coarse paste. Alternatively, pound them with a mortar and pestle. You may need to add a little water to bring the paste together, but try to add as little as possible, as the ingredients (particularly the soaked chillies and shrimp) contain their own moisture.

Heat the pork fat (or vegetable oil) in a heavy-based pan and add the chilli paste. You need to cook it very slowly, taking care that it doesn't catch on the bottom of the pan, for about 2 hours – yes 2 hours! – until all the moisture has disappeared. After an hour or so, add the palm sugar and 1 tablespoon of the fish sauce. When the chilli jam is ready, it will have become very aromatic and the colour will have deepened to a rich red-brown. At this point you can take it off the heat and keep it on one side until you are ready to fry the partridges.

Strip the birds of their meat and cut it into finger-sized pieces. Heat a wok with a little vegetable oil, add the partridge and fry until it starts to get a little colour and the skin becomes crisp. Stir in the gai lan or broccoli. Add a good couple of spoons of chilli jam and toss well. Add a few drops of fish sauce and continue cooking until it is thoroughly heated – it should be sticky, hot and sweet. Scatter the dish with lime leaves, Thai basil and some deep-fried garlic and chilli slices, and it's ready to serve.

Tip: The best Thai fish sauce is the Squid brand, which you can buy for the equivalent of a few pence in Thailand, and is exported relatively cheaply in big bottles that will keep for quite a long time, letting the sauce darken and mature gently.

A barbecue is not just for summer. Nor is it about burnt food, boys and beer. Barbecuing is a wonderful way to cook, but one that needs a bit of practice, an understanding of coals and flames, and patience. Barbies can be a little special too. Why not set a table outside and welcome your friends with a glass of champagne?

You can barbecue all year round. It may feel a little unnatural the first time you stand outside wearing a hat and gloves while cooking, but imagine the joy, the romance of eating summery-flavoured barbecued chicken or duck as the snow falls outside – with the added benefit of having no smoke in the kitchen.

When cooking over coals remember: if there are flames, it ain't ready. Cooking a piece of chicken, duck or turkey is not quick if you want it to be beautifully smoky, crisp outside and moist and soft inside. The trick is to find the hot spots and cool spots. Some things you want to sear over a high heat, others you want to put over a high heat to get some colour and then move to a slightly cooler (but still hot) area to cook through. For more on barbecuing chicken breast and leg pieces, see page 62.

barbecue

BARBECUING KEBABS

The idea of making up some little skewers, or even big skewers, and cooking them quickly on the barbecue is a good one. Various things can be used to spear your ingredients: rosemary twigs, bamboo sticks, big metal skewers – you can even cook little marinated hunks on toothpicks and serve them as a canapé.

Whatever you choose, always soak any wood or herb branch in water for at least 10 minutes before threading the meat on it for barbecuing – this will stop it bursting into flames.

Aim to marinate the raw poultry for a good few hours to let the flavours soak in and remember to keep a bit of the marinade back to brush over the food while it is on the barbecue.

When you're ready to cook, make sure that your barbecue coals are glowing but there is no flame. When you are using a griddle plate, just keep the heat around medium. If it is all too hot, your chunks of meat will be burnt on the outside but not cooked through, and we don't want that.

All the recipes that follow simply use thigh or breast meat. In general I prefer the former. Keep the skin on when using lean breast meat – the flesh needs protecting from the intense and direct heat if it is to stay moist. You can always remove the skin on serving.

It's common to cut poultry into cubes about 2 or 3cm square but there are exceptions, such as satay, which is traditionally cut in strips. For this you need to thread the meat on the skewers so that the maximum amount of flesh is exposed – that way, when the skewers are put on the hot barbecue they cook quickly and the flesh stays moist and tender.

OREGANO AND GARLIC

10 garlic cloves
1 tsp salt
1 tsp freshly ground black pepper
120ml olive oil
1 handful oregano, finely chopped
6 chicken thighs or breasts, with skin

Crush the garlic to a paste and season well with salt and pepper. Mix in the olive oil followed by the oregano. Cut the chicken into 2cm cubes, add to the flavoured oil and mix well. Leave to marinate for 20 minutes.

Thread about six hunks of chicken on each of twelve skewers – this is a good time to use branches of rosemary. Place on the barbecue and cook, turning every 3 minutes and rotating the kebabs at least four times so that all the meat is well coloured. Great with spiced couscous and a big salad. MAKES 12.

CHICKEN TIKKA

6 chicken breasts, with skin, cut into 4 strips
juice of 1 lemon
1 large pinch salt
1 tsp turmeric powder
2 dried red chillies, or 1 tsp chilli powder
1 tsp cumin seeds
1/2 tsp coriander seeds
1 pinch asafoetida
a little white pepper
200ml yoghurt

Put the chicken in a bowl and cover with the lemon juice and salt. To make the paste, toast the spices in a hot dry pan until fragrant and about to smoke. Crush to a powder and combine with the yoghurt. Drain the lemon juice from the chicken, then pour the spiced yoghurt over the chicken and rub it in well.

Thread two strips of chicken on each skewer so that they are long rather than bunched up. Cook on the hot barbecue for 3 minutes, then turn and brush the cooked portion with some of the leftover yoghurt marinade. Continue cooking, turning and brushing for about 12 minutes in total, then serve the tikkas with flatbread. MAKES 12.

CHICKEN AND PRAWNS WITH PANCETTA

1 garlic clove, chopped
100ml olive oil
juice and pared rind of 1 lemon
24 large raw prawns, peeled and deveined
6 large skinless chicken breasts, each cut into eight
24 slices pancetta
48 basil leaves
salt and pepper
lemon wedges and mayonnaise, to serve

Mix the garlic, oil, lemon juice and rind and some salt and pepper in a bowl. Add the prawns and marinate for at least 10 minutes, then add the chicken.

Lay a piece of pancetta on a work surface and place a basil leaf on top. Lay a prawn on top, then another basil leaf. Take the end of the pancetta and wrap it round the prawn. Repeat until all the prawns are wrapped.

Take a large metal skewer and thread a piece of chicken on it, followed by a wrapped prawn and another piece of chicken. Repeat so that you have four bits of chicken and two prawns on each skewer.

Cook on a hot barbecue, turning regularly, for about 10 minutes. Serve with lemon and mayo. MAKES 12.

SATAY

100ml light soy sauce
200ml mirin
100g miso paste
500g skinless chicken fillets, cut into 5mm strips
PEANUT SAUCE
1 shallot, diced
50ml vegetable oil
1 tbsp Thai red curry paste
2 small red chillies, deseeded and finely chopped
300g freshly ground peanuts or crunchy peanut butter
50ml soy sauce
1 large handful chopped coriander

For the sauce: fry the shallot in oil for 3 minutes. Add the curry paste and chillies. Cook, stirring, for 5 minutes until fragrant. Mix in the ground peanuts and 200ml water. Bring to the boil, add the soy sauce and set aside.

For the satays: mix together the soy sauce, mirin and miso then stir in the chicken and leave for 20 minutes. Thread on skewers and place on the hot barbecue. Cook, turning every 30 seconds or so. They should only take a couple of minutes. Stir the coriander into the sauce and serve with the satay. SERVES 4-6.

PAPRIKA CHICKEN WITH FENNEL, TOMATO & PARSLEY SALAD

3 plum tomatoes,
1 bulb fennel, thinly shaved
100g black olives, stones removed
juice of 1 lemon
olive oil
6 chicken breasts, with skin, cut into 3-5cm chunks
2 garlic cloves, crushed
2 tsp hot smoked paprika
1 large handful flat-leaf parsley, roughly chopped
salt and pepper

Take the tomatoes and chop them roughly, squeezing out as much juice and goodness as possible. Put them in a large mixing bowl with the fennel, olives, lemon juice, 20ml olive oil and a good pinch of salt, and mix with vigour. Set aside.

Mix the chicken with 50ml olive oil, the garlic, paprika and a good amount of salt and pepper. Thread the meat on skewers and lay on the hot barbecue. Cook for 15 minutes, turning every couple of minutes until lightly charred on each side. Stir the parsley through the salad and serve with the kebabs. Some extra grilled veg on the side is lovely. SERVES 6

GREEN CURRY

6 chicken breast fillets, with skin
400g can coconut milk
2 tbsp green curry paste, bought or home-made
    (page 112)
1 handful chopped coriander

Cut the breasts into even-sized pieces. Mix the coconut milk with the green curry paste and the chopped coriander. Add the chicken and leave to marinate for a few hours or overnight.

Thread the chicken on skewers. Lay them skin-side down over glowing coals or on a hot griddle plate. Cook for 3 to 4 minutes then turn over cook for 3 to 4 minutes on the other side. Turn again, cooking each side for a further 3 minutes. Remove from the heat and cover with a plate to keep warm until the rest of your food is ready. SERVES 6.

CHINESE CHICKEN WITH SESAME SEEDS

This is a simple and ever-useful marinade that can be used for chunks, hunks or even whole breasts of chicken.

50ml honey
50ml soy sauce
50ml sherry
2 spring onions, thinly sliced
50ml oyster sauce
20ml tomato ketchup
50g sesame seeds
6 skinless chicken breasts, cut into 3 strips

In a saucepan, heat the honey with the soy sauce and sherry. Once it is starting to boil, remove from the heat, add the spring onions and allow to cool a little. Add the ketchup and oyster sauce, stir well, then add the sesame seeds. Marinate the chicken in this mixture for at least 10 minutes before threading it on skewers and barbecuing.

Return the remaining marinade to the saucepan and bring to the boil. When the chicken is cooked, spoon the marinade over the cooked chicken. Serve with lettuce cups, some more spring onions and a few napkins per person. SERVES 6.

SPICED YOGHURT

10 chicken thigh fillets, with skin
juice of 2 lemons
3 sprigs thyme, picked
250ml yoghurt
2 red chillies, deseeded
2 garlic cloves
2 tbsp chopped coriander
1 large pinch ground cinnamon
1 large pinch ground cardamom
1 large pinch ground cloves
1 large pinch turmeric powder
salt and pepper

You first need to tenderize the chicken by rubbing it with a mixture of the lemon juice, 1 tablespoon of salt, and the thyme leaves. Leave for a few hours. When ready to proceed, put the yoghurt, chillies, garlic, coriander and dry spices in a food processor and blend to make a paste. Rub this all over the chicken and leave to marinate (preferably overnight). Thread on skewers and barbecue, turning regularly, for about 20 minutes so that the chicken is well charred. Serve with skordalia (page 80), flatbread and tzatziki. SERVES 6.

SPATCHCOCK POUSSIN WITH GARLIC

SERVES 🐔🐔🐔🐔🐔🐔🐔🐔🐔🐔

3 tbsp salt
1 tbsp ground black pepper
100ml olive oil
10 spatchcocked poussins,
  or 3 large spatchcocked
  chickens
1 handful rosemary sprigs
40 garlic cloves (yes 40!)

I believe that poultry needs a little fat for flavour and crispy skin for both flavour and texture, but I also understand that not everyone likes the fat. This dish satisfies both ways of thinking: the fat melts away while the meat is cooking and the skin goes crisp.

If possible the night before cooking, mix together the salt, pepper and olive oil. Poke the birds with a sharp knife making slits just big enough to fit a clove of garlic in each – so about 4 slits in each poussin, more if you're using chicken.

Don't fill the slits with garlic yet, you'll do that the next day or later on. Rub the seasoned olive oil over the birds, cover well and place in the refrigerator, preferably overnight but for at least 1 hour.

When ready to proceed, peel the garlic and cut the rosemary into 2cm long pieces. Put one whole garlic clove and a bit of rosemary in each slit you made in the poultry.

Get your barbecue coals or griddle plate nice and hot, then place the birds, rosemary and garlic side-down over the heat and cook for approximately 10 minutes until well coloured. Turn so that the rosemary and garlic sits up and cook for a further 10 minutes until well coloured, then cover the barbecue and cook for another 10 minutes or so on each side. Serve with a salad of avocado, baby spinach and pine nuts.

MINCED CHICKEN ON LEMONGRASS

MAKES

12 stalks lemongrass
4 coriander roots, chopped
7 white peppercorns, crushed
2 Thai shallots, very finely
  sliced
2 tsp fish sauce
1 large egg white
1 lime leaf, finely shredded
300g minced chicken

This is one of those recipes that Thais disagree about. Some say the 'real' recipe calls for the chicken to be wrapped around sugar cane rather than lemongrass, so the sugar cane gives a caramel sweetness to the chicken. Either way, it tastes great.

Trim the lemongrass at both ends to create a stick about the same length as a pencil. Peel away about four layers, bruise the stalks well to release their flavour and soak in water for approximately 10 minutes. Meanwhile, pound the coriander roots and peppercorns together in a mortar to form a paste.

Mix all the other ingredients together in a large bowl. Divide the mixture into twelve pieces and shape one around the end of each stalk of lemongrass. Barbecue gently for about 15 minutes, turning frequently and occasionally splashing the chicken with water to keep it moist.

SPICED CHICKEN PATTIE WITH TOMATO SALSA

SERVES

1 knob ginger, peeled
1 garlic clove
4 white peppercorns, or some
  ground white pepper
1 handful coriander sprigs
1 tsp vegetable oil
500g minced chicken
2 handfuls fresh white
  breadcrumbs
2 eggs, beaten

SALSA
2 tbsp vegetable oil
2 tsp ground cumin
1 tsp ground coriander
1 tsp turmeric powder
1 onion
1 garlic clove, crushed
300ml tomato passata or
  chopped tinned tomatoes
salt and pepper

These little beauties are full of ginger and spice, but should not be too overpowering as you still want to taste the chicken. The recipe works just as well with turkey. I love the spicy sauce and it should be served with these bad boys and a good handful of wild rocket in a soft floury bap.

Pound the ginger, garlic, white pepper and coriander together to make a paste, then add the oil. Mix the chicken, breadcrumbs, eggs, spice paste and some salt together with your hands in a large bowl until well combined.

Shape into six balls and flatten them into patties. Chill for 2 hours before cooking so that the mixture has a chance to set.

To make the salsa, heat the oil in a frying pan. Add the spices and cook for 1 minute, then add the onion and stir constantly for a few minutes until the onion is translucent. Add the garlic and cook for a further minute. Pour in the tomato passata or crushed tomatoes and bring to the boil. Cook for 10 minutes and season well with salt and pepper.

Barbecue the patties for 10 minutes, turning halfway through cooking, and serve with the salsa, in baps if desired.

CHICKEN BURGERS

SERVES 🐔🐔🐔🐔🐔🐔🐔🐔

1 medium onion, roughly
  chopped
1 large handful flat-leaf parsley
2 tbsp tomato ketchup
1 tbsp oyster sauce
600g sausage meat
600g minced chicken
1 egg plus 1 egg yolk

TO SERVE
8 rashers smoked bacon
8 eggs (optional)
8 burger buns
8 slices good melting cheese
1 jar tomato relish

You want barbecued burgers to be big and juicy. I try to use quality sausage mince with a good amount of fat through it and beat in a little water to keep it really moist. My other little secret is to use Chinese oyster sauce instead of salt to season the mixture.

Put the onion, parsley, ketchup and oyster sauce in a food processor and blend to a paste. Combine the sausage meat and minced chicken in a mixing bowl and beat in the onion mixture, whole egg and egg yolk, plus 50ml of water – and I mean really beat it. Divide the mix into eight and roll into large balls. Put them in the fridge to chill for a good hour.

To cook the burgers, either have the barbecue good and hot with the coals glowing or heat a griddle plate over a medium heat. Do not add any oil at all. Place the burgers on the barbecue and leave for a few minutes, until the edges start to colour. Turn over and cook for a few more minutes. Turn them again and, if you're using a griddle plate reduce the heat, or if you're using a coal barbecue move the burgers to the side or a place where the heat is less intense and cook for a good 15 minutes if you would like them well done.

While the burgers are cooking, fry some bacon and, if you are game, some eggs as well – I love burgers and eggs. Cut your burger buns in half and toast them lightly on the cut sides.

Stack the burgers and bacon on the bases. Top with a slice of cheese and place under a grill to melt the cheese. Toast the tops of the buns and spread with loads of butter and add a good spoonful of tomato relish. Sit your fried eggs (if using) on top of the melted cheese, cover with the top half of the buns and serve each with a wooden skewer through the middle to hold it all together. Don't forget the linen napkins.

JERK CHICKEN

SERVES

12 chicken thighs, bone in,
or 8 large chicken breasts

MARINADE
1 large bunch spring onions, or
2 smaller bunches
2 tbsp soy sauce
2 tbsp vegetable oil
1 tbsp salt
juice of 1 lime
1/2 tsp dried thyme, or 1 tbsp
fresh thyme
1 tbsp allspice berries
1-10 scotch bonnets (start with
a small amount and add
more later if you think it
needs it)
1 thumb-sized piece ginger
3 garlic cloves
1/2 small onion
2-3 tbsp of brown sugar

To get a more authentic jerk experience, add some wood chips to your barbecue and cook your chicken thighs or legs over slow indirect heat for the best flavour. Alternatively enjoy a beautiful jerk chicken breast cooked over a high heat – it should be ready in 10 minutes or less.

To make the marinade, put all the ingredients in a blender and process until you have a purée. Don't add more water if you're having trouble getting it all blended, just keep turning off the blender, stirring it up with a spatula, and trying again. Eventually it will start to blend up nicely. Now taste it. It should taste pretty salty, but not unpleasantly puckeringly salty. You can also now throw in more chillies if it's not spicy enough for you. If you think it tastes too salty and sour, try adding a bit more brown sugar until things seem good and balanced.

Put the chicken pieces in a bowl, cover with the marinade and leave overnight. Next day, cook the chicken over a smoky fire for 15 to 20 minutes, turning about six times during cooking.

RICE & PEAS

SERVES 🐔 🐔 🐔 🐔 🐔 🐔 🐔 🐔

250g long grain rice
125g basmati rice
100g coconut cream
2 large white onions, finely
  chopped
1 ham or bacon bone with a bit
  of meat left on it
2 bushy thyme sprigs
1 scotch bonnet chilli, left
  whole
40g saltfish, soaked in water
  overnight (optional)
400g can coconut milk
400g can red kidney beans or
  black-eyed beans, drained
500ml chicken stock or ham
  stock
salt and pepper

Mix the two rices together, wash them thoroughly and leave to drain. In a casserole, melt the coconut cream, add the onions and fry gently until transparent. Add the ham bone, thyme, chilli and saltfish, if using. Add the rice and coconut milk and bring slowly to a simmer.

Add the drained beans and half the stock and return the pot to a simmer. Turn the heat right down to its lowest possible setting, season with salt and pepper then cover and leave to cook gently for 20-30 minutes, stirring occasionally and adding more stock as necessary.

When the rice is cooked, turn off the heat and leave it to stand with the lid on for 10 minutes. Discard the ham bone, thyme and chilli before serving.

BUFFALO WINGS & DRUMSTICKS

SERVES

200ml tomato ketchup
100ml light soy sauce
100ml olive oil
50ml Worcestershire sauce
20ml Tabasco sauce (optional)
1 garlic clove, crushed
1 egg yolk
12 chicken wings
12 chicken drumsticks

The Americans are mad about buffalo wings but in Britain we seem to think that they are just skin and fat. The truth is that chicken wings are very tasty. They have a lot of skin, but that skin cooks to be crisp and delicious, especially when the wings have been left in a quality marinade for a good period. The joy of sucking the meat from the wings fresh from the barbie is great and once cooled, the kids will love them – they are allowed to use their fingers after all.

The night before, mix together the ketchup, soy sauce, olive oil, Worcestershire sauce, Tabasco (if using) and garlic. Stir well, then mix in the egg yolk. Clean the wings and drumsticks of any feathers or yucky bits, drop them in the marinade and leave overnight. If short on time, try to marinate them for a few hours at least.

Heat your barbecue and once the coals are white with a little ash, place the wings and drumsticks on it. If using a gas barbecue, turn it up high to get it really hot, then reduce the heat to medium once you've put on the chicken pieces. Leave for a few minutes, then start to move them around. If the barbecue starts to flare, take the chicken pieces off briefly or move them more often – this is just a result of the fat being broken down. I cook wings and drumsticks for a good 20 minutes so the outsides are well coloured and the skin is starting to crisp.

Once cooked, pile the chicken up on a large flat plate and have a few finger bowls and plenty of napkins at the ready.

GREEK-STYLE CHICKEN WITH FETA, TOMATOES AND OLIVES

SERVES 🐔 🐔 🐔 🐔 🐔 🐔 🐔 🐔 🐔 🐔

12 chicken thighs fillets, skin on
10 garlic cloves, crushed
1 tsp flaky sea salt
1 handful picked rosemary
juice of 2 lemons
200ml olive oil
1 large handful flat-leaf parsley
1 large handful oregano or
   marjoram
100g plum tomatoes
200g black pitted olives
200g feta cheese

The Greeks are clever cooks who use lesser cuts of high-quality meat for flavour but also marinate them to tenderise the flesh. This recipe is a prime example.

Use a sharp knife to score the skin of the chicken, then lay the thighs out flat in a large dish ready to marinate. Mix together the garlic, salt, rosemary, lemon juice and 100ml of the olive oil. Pour over the chicken, rubbing well. Leave for an hour or so.

In a food processor, blend the parsley and oregano or marjoram with the remaining 100ml of olive oil. Pour half this mixture over the chicken and give it a good stir.

Cut the tomatoes into little chunks about the size of dice and mix with the olives and remaining herb oil. Set aside.

Barbecue the marinated chicken thighs, giving them a good blast of heat for 2 minutes before turning. Lift them a little higher away from the coals, or move to a less intense part of the griddle, and cook for 15 minutes or so turning often.

When the chicken is cooked, place it on a large flat serving dish. Sprinkle with the tomato, olive and herb mixture then crumble over the feta cheese and serve.

STUFFED CHICKEN WITH OLIVES AND ARTICHOKES

SERVES

1 knob butter

1 large leek

olive oil, for drizzling

6 large chicken breasts, skin on

100g mixed olives, stones removed

100g artichokes packed in olive oil

1 red chilli, deseeded and finely chopped

200g ricotta or feta cheese

1 egg

1 lemon, halved or quartered

salt and pepper

Serve a good salad as a starter and then this terrific chicken with some extra artichokes and olives.

Bring a pot of water to the boil with the butter and some salt and pepper. Clean the leek, splitting it down the centre to make long flat strips, and plunge into the boiling water. Leave to cook for 3 minutes, then drain and run under cold water to cool. Put the leek in a bowl, pour over some olive oil, season and leave to sit.

Lay a chicken breast on the work surface with the skin-side up and the pointed end of the breast closest to you. Take a sharp knife and cut the chicken from the top right hand side all the way down the side, so that the breast can be opened out to resemble a butterfly. Keeping the knife parallel to the board should make it a little easier. Repeat the process until all the breasts are done, and lay them out ready to be filled.

Squash the olives and remove any remnants of stone. Chop the artichokes but not too finely. Mix the olives and artichokes with the chilli and ricotta or feta to make the filling. In a separate small bowl, beat the egg and set aside.

Take a decent spoonful of the filling and place on the centre of each open chicken breast. Brush the edges of each breast well with beaten egg and fold the chicken up to make a parcel, tucking in all the edges so the stuffing is not exposed.

Lay two pieces of leek flat and place a filled chicken breast on top. Wrap the leeks around it and secure the ends of the leeks to the breast with a few toothpicks. Repeat until all the filled chicken breasts are wrapped.

Put the parcels on the barbecue and cook for 5 minutes on either side, then repeat so they cook for about 20 minutes in total. Before serving, squeeze some lemon juice over them, sprinkle with ground black pepper and drizzle with olive oil.

BARBECUED DUCK

SERVES

1 duck, all bones removed (you
    may need to get your butcher
    to do this)
1 jar hoisin sauce

**Duck is a funny one on the barbecue as it has a good
amount of fat in it that needs to be melted and the meat
needs to be cooked slowly or it will be tough. This dish
is inspired by the Asians and the way they can get any
meat, whether it be tough or tender, to eat beautifully.**

Take a 10-litre pot and three-quarters fill it with cold water. Stir
in the hoisin sauce then put the duck in and turn the heat to
medium. Slowly bring the water to the boil – it should take a
good 20 to 30 minutes. As soon as it is boiling, turn the heat
down and cook gently for 15 minutes. Switch off the heat and
leave the duck to cool for 3 hours in the water. Lift the duck out
and pat it dry with kitchen paper.

Heat your barbecue. Lay the duck on it, skin-side down, and
cook until it starts to colour. Turn the duck over and cook for a
good 5 minutes. Repeat until the duck is cooked well on both
sides – the outside should be crisp and the flesh soft inside.

Take the duck from the barbecue, carve and serve garnished with
spring onions. Alternatively, it's good sliced very thinly and
served in a wrap with some tomatoes, shredded spring onions
and coriander leaves.

As I have already said, if you can roast a chicken you can survive. Roasting is one of the seven principles of cooking and once mastered, such a useful skill. All ovens are different and I have given guides on temperatures and times and of course my recipes do work, but you will also need to feel your way a little.

The first rule of roasting is that whatever you roast needs to have oil or fat to conduct the heat and keep the bird moist. The second and only other rule is all about the oven: once at temperature and once the bird and all its accompanying bits are in, *shut the bloody door*. I say it all the time. Every time you open the door the cold air goes in and the temperature drops and slows down the cooking process. More importantly, if you are roasting a whole bird you rely on the bones to conduct the heat and the cold air rushing in chills the bones so the heat does not get in deep. The result is a dry, over-cooked exterior and breast and under-cooked legs and thighs. Try to open the door only when really necessary, when something needs to be added to your roast, or if it's on fire! Get it? *Shut the bloody door.*

roasts

CHICKEN WITH OLIVES AND LEMONS

SERVES

1 very large chicken
3 whole lemons, quartered
24 green and purple giant
   olives
1kg new potatoes
60ml olive oil
salt and pepper

This is a very easy but satisfying, full-of-flavour roast chicken.

Heat the oven to 170°C (gas 3). Season the chicken inside and out with salt and pepper and fill the cavity with most of the lemons and olives. Give it a good shake.

Take a very big cast-iron pot and put the potatoes in the bottom. Mix the oil with the rest of the lemons and olives and squash them a bit. Put the chook in the pot on top of the potatoes and pour the oil and lemon mixture over it, letting the bits roll off onto the spuds. Season well then put the pot in the oven and shut the door for at least 1½ hours.

Check the chicken is cooked by sticking a skewer between the legs and breast: if the juice that runs out is clear it is cooked, otherwise put it back in the oven.

When done, lift the chicken from the pot and pour all the bits from inside the cavity over the potatoes. Place the pot over a very high heat and bring to the boil while you cut the chicken into big hunks. Add the chicken pieces back to the pot along with any juices, turn off the heat and take the whole lot to the table.

BEST EVER ROAST CHICKEN (CHOOK)

SERVES

1 handful sage leaves
1 handful marjoram sprigs
2 branches thyme, leaves
  picked
100g softened butter
2 chickens, about 1.5kg each
your choice of stuffing (pages
  164-168)
50ml olive oil
6 large potatoes, peeled and
  cut into chunks
salt and black pepper

Oh, oh, oh, I am the biggest sucker for chicken. I am an even bigger sucker for chicken that has a good stuffing. For those who like to cook delicious food but keep it simple, this is a gem, as the potatoes, stuffing and chicken are all ready to eat at once, and the juices left behind make the best-ever gravy.

Heat the oven to 180°C (gas 4). Chop all the herbs roughly and mix them with the softened butter, salt and pepper. Fill the chickens with your preferred stuffing and place one-third of the herb butter in the end cavity of each chicken so the butter melts inside the bird.

Place a high-sided roasting tin over a high heat and add the oil. Drop in the potatoes and shake well to coat them in oil. Put the chickens in with the potatoes, pushing them out of the way. Place the roasting tray in the oven and leave to cook for 35 minutes without opening the door.

Remove the tray from the oven and increase the temperature to 190°C (gas 5). Turn the potatoes over and baste the birds well, spooning the pan juices over the breasts. Return to the oven and leave to cook for a further 40 minutes, at which point the chicken and potatoes should be done.

CARVING A ROAST BIRD

The secret to carving any bird is confidence and a little understanding of how the bird is put together. You do have to practice, however, so cook a chook a week and in three weeks you will be a master!

First, in your mind's eye, split the bird in half. Half a bird – be it chicken, duck, turkey or whatever – has from back to front a wing and wing joint, the breast, a leg and a thigh. Some people like the brown meat from the leg, thigh and wing, and some like the white meat from the breast. Regardless of what you may think, the breast meat is the only part of the bird that needs to be sliced because anyone who likes the brown meat is very happy to chew on the bones.

Take the bird and, using a long, sharp knife, make a cut in between the thigh and the pointy end of the breast. Using the flat of the blade, push the leg away and let the skin tear naturally – the leg should just pop out and you will be left with a good amount of skin on the breast. Turn the bird around and cut between the wing and the fat end of the breast. Chop these bits any way you like – I separate the thigh from the leg and serve them to those whose hand is up quickest; I also separate the fat wing section from the pinions – the end bits are always mine, because they have lots of bones and delicious brown meat.

Now if you do that on both sides of the bird you will be left with what in the professional kitchen we call the crown. Take long thin slices of breast – use a long, thin knife and cut with confidence and you should be fine. If you leave too much meat on the bone, give the carcass to those who had their hand up for the legs and didn't get one – they will usually nibble on it happily.

CHICKEN GRAVY

The best gravy is always made from the roasting tin of the best roast chicken. To be successful you need to take the chicken out when it has cooled a little and carefully drain any juice from it – you can also prick the underside of the roast chicken a few times to drain out any of the good stuff.

Drain off most of the fat but be sure to leave some, then put the roasting tin over a medium heat and add two dessertspoons of flour. Stir well and let it cook for a few minutes, then add a couple of pinches of salt and a little pepper.

Take a good litre of water and add half to the roasting tin, stirring well. Bring to the boil, scraping all the caramelised bits off the bottom of the tin, and making sure there are no lumps. Add the rest of the water (you may need some more, that's fine) and bring the gravy to the boil again. Cook for a few minutes more, stirring and stirring. Pour the gravy into a warmed jug and serve. That's it – the first thing I learned to cook, aged five.

MASHED POTATO

SERVES

2kg potatoes, peeled
100g butter
200ml milk
salt and white pepper

I think really good mash has to be piping-hot and beaten quite hard until it is creamy and peaky but still has the texture of a good floury potato. There are many theories about how mash should be cooked, so here I am giving you some important basic principles. You can't really make hard-and-fast rules, you've got to understand the feel of the potato. I may well use only 8 tablespoons of milk and 25g butter, but I'll start with a little of each and add more, depending on how much the potato takes up.

Cut the potatoes into equal sized pieces so they cook at the same rate or in the same amount of time. Cover with plenty of cold salted water (I use a generous pinch of Maldon salt), bring to the boil over a medium heat and cook gently so the water is just moving. When you can easily slip a knife through the potato, drain well. Return the potatoes to the pan and place back on the heat to evaporate the excess moisture.

Mash well with a masher or a fork (I prefer a fork but many do not). Keep the heat going under the pan to evaporate any moisture that may appear when the potatoes are mashed. Season well, add the butter and mix in roughly. Add the milk and beat continuously over the heat until the mixture starts to bubble. Add more milk and butter as you like; if you want to add a touch of cream, fine, but I prefer not to. Taste and season again. Serve with something as good and as simple.

BREAD SAUCE

SERVES 🐔🐔🐔🐔🐔🐔🐔🐔🐔🐔

500ml milk
1 medium onion, peeled and
   halved
6 black peppercorns
2 whole cloves
1 small blade mace, or 1 pinch
   freshly grated nutmeg
120g fresh white breadcrumbs
30g butter
sea salt

Once you have served your bread sauce, soak the pan in water as the remains can set and be difficult to remove come washing-up time.

Put the milk in a saucepan with the onion, spices and salt and place over a medium heat. When the milk comes to a simmer, remove from the heat and leave to infuse, ideally for 1 hour but 15 minutes will do.

Warm the milk again and add the breadcrumbs and butter, stirring well. Let the sauce cook for a few minutes. When ready, it should have body and thickness – a bit like porridge. If it is too thick, add a little more milk; if too thin, continue cooking until some liquid evaporates to give the desired consistency.

A QUICK RECIPE FOR CARROTS

SERVES

100g butter
12 small carrots, scrubbed or
   peeled
1 tsp brown sugar
salt and pepper

Melt the butter in a heavy pan, add 100ml water and season well. Add the carrots and cook over a medium heat for 10 minutes, or until they have softened and the majority of the water has evaporated. Add the sugar, stir well and continue to cook for 2 minutes until the sugar has dissolved.

GREEN PEA PURÉE

SERVES

600g frozen peas
3 spring onions, chopped
50g butter
100ml double cream

Put a kettle of water on to boil. Put the peas in a medium-sized saucepan and cover with 200ml boiled water. Place over a high heat, add the spring onions and butter, and bring to the boil. Cook for 3 minutes. Add the cream and return to the boil.

Remove the pan from the heat. Blend the pea mixture in a food processor for 1 minute or so, until smooth.

TURKEY WITH CARAMELISED ONIONS

SERVES 🐔🐔🐔🐔🐔🐔🐔

4.5kg turkey
100g salted butter
2 tsp sea salt
2 tsp ground black pepper
3 large onions

I wasn't particularly interested in turkey until I met Paul Kelly and started to appreciate what this gem is all about and why it is one of America's greatest exports outside peanut butter. Make sure you have a roasting tin large enough to fit your turkey and a trivet to cook it on – I use a cake cooling rack.

The night before roasting, soften the butter and add half the salt and half the pepper, mixing well. Remove the giblets from the bird and wipe it inside and out with kitchen paper. Remove any feathers – if there are a lot you can singe them over a gas flame.

Open the cavity of the bird and season the inside with the remaining salt and pepper. Rub the seasoned butter over the turkey. Take a piece of greaseproof paper twice the size of the breast and fold to give a double layer. Lay this over the breasts (it will protect them during the cooking) and return the turkey to the fridge until morning.

Calculate your cooking times – allow 20 minutes at high heat, then 30 minutes per kilo after that. A 4.5kg turkey will therefore take approximately 2½ hours to cook in total.

Heat the oven to 220°C (gas 7). Take the turkey from the fridge and allow it to come to room temperature while the oven is heating up.

Cut the onions in half and place in the roasting tin. Sit the turkey on a trivet inside the tin. Bring a kettle of water to the boil and carefully pour around 250ml of the hot water into the cavity of the bird. Seal with a skewer. Pour another 500ml of hot water into the roasting tray with the onions. Cover the whole thing with foil (I use two layers) and make sure that it is well sealed around the edges.

Put the lot in the oven and cook for 20 minutes, then reduce the temperature to 200°C (gas 6) for the remaining cooking time. After 1½ hours, remove the foil and the greaseproof paper and close the door. Don't open it again until the cooking time is up.

To test whether the turkey is cooked, insert a skewer or knife blade into the point where the thigh joins the breast. The juice should run clear; if it is pink, then roast the turkey for another 20 minutes and test again.

Take the bird from the oven and leave it to rest in a warm place for at least 30 minutes. Strain the juice from the bottom of the roasting tin into a large jug to settle. The fat will rise to the top, leaving the aromatic turkey and onion juice beneath. Skim off the fat and thicken the juices if you wish, or serve them as is.

Who is going to carve the turkey when it gets to the table, if indeed it gets that far? Well here are some helpful words from a very old edition of *Eliza Acton's Cookery and Household Management*: 'A turkey does not call for greater skill in carving than a fowl. The first thing to do is to cut a succession of long slices from the breast, each with its nice little edge of untorn skin. The cutting of slices from the breast should begin as close to the wing as possible, and proceed upwards to the ridge of the breast bone.'

She goes on to say that: 'The serving of the wings and the legs is only on rare occasions necessary at table, as the breast of the bird usually yields an ample supply for an average amount of guests. But in the event of the carver being called on to disjoint a wing or leg, it is done the same way as with a chicken.'

STUFFING

50g butter
1 large onion, diced
100g bacon, roughly chopped
200g cooked chestnuts, finely
    chopped
150g fresh breadcrumbs
grated zest of 1 lemon
1 handful flat-leaf parsley,
    roughly chopped
salt and pepper

There are two schools of thought on stuffing. One is that the stuffing should be put in the neck end of the bird, near the wishbone. The other is that the stuffing should be cooked separately. Personally, I agree with the latter, because the type of stuffing I prefer is quite dense and doesn't necessarily cook well inside the bird. Also, stuffing slows the roasting time. Cooking the stuffing separately puts you in control of the cooking time, and results in crispy topping and sides and a lovely moist centre. You can make this good old fashioned chestnut and bacon stuffing, and the ones on the following pages, the day before roasting.

In a frying pan, melt the butter over a high heat and add a pinch of salt and two grinds from the pepper mill. Add the onion and cook until translucent. Add the bacon and cook for another 5 minutes, stirring often so not to burn the onion.

Add the chestnuts, then remove from the heat and add the breadcrumbs, lemon zest and parsley. Taste and if necessary add more salt and pepper so that it is seasoned thoroughly.

Grease a 30 x 10cm ovenproof dish and spoon the stuffing in (don't pat it down). Cook at 200°C (gas 6) for about 40 minutes until crisp on top, then serve with your roast dinner.

POSH PEAR

1kg conference pears, peeled
375ml inexpensive white wine
2 cinnamon sticks
2 cloves
1 pork tenderloin, minced
finely grated zest of 1 lemon
200g fresh breadcrumbs
a few sage leaves, chopped
2 junpier berries, crushed
1 egg

Put the pears, wine, cinnamon and cloves in a saucepan and bring to the boil. Remove from the heat and leave to cool.

Once cool, chop or even slice the pears if you want to to be really posh, discarding the cores and stems. Mix with the rest of the ingredients, using a little of the pear cooking liquid to make it all moist, but bear in mind this mixture is crumbly!

SPICED CRANBERRY & APPLE

5 bramley apples, peeled and chopped
2 cloves
50g sugar
1 tsp vinegar
1 bay leaf
300g frozen cranberries, defrosted
2 large shallots, diced
2 cloves garlic, crushed
50g butter
300g turkey or chicken, minced
100g fresh breadcrumbs soaked in a little milk
1 egg
2 pinches allspice powder
salt and pepper

Put the apples, cloves, sugar, vinegar and bay leaf in a saucepan and cook over a low heat until soft but not mushy. Drop in the cranberries, discard the cloves and set aside.

In another pan, cook the shallots and garlic in the butter until soft, then stir them into the minced turkey or chicken. Combine the two mixtures, then add the rest of the ingredients and slap to a stuffing.

SAGE AND APPLE

2 large potatoes, peeled and chopped
2 onions, chopped
2 parsnips, peeled and chopped
50g butter
2 granny smith apples, peeled and chopped
1 handful mixture chopped sage and parsley
50g fresh breadcrumbs
100g pork sausage meat
1 egg
salt and pepper

Boil the potatoes, onions and parsnips until soft, then drain. Melt the butter in a pan then add the veg and fry for 1 minute. Season really well, adding lots of pepper. Stir in the apples and leave to cool. Mix in all the rest of the bits, then taste and adjust the seasoning as you wish.

BOOZY REDCURRANT & ORANGE

1 onion, diced
100g butter
100g bacon, chopped or cut into lardons
50ml brandy or calvados
200g pork sausage meat
150g fresh breadcrumbs
300g redcurrants
½ orange, rind and flesh chopped separately
finely grated rind of ½ lemon
1 small bunch parsley, finely chopped
½ nutmeg, grated
1 egg
50ml milk
salt and pepper

Sweat the onion in the butter. When it is tender, add the bacon and fry it quickly. Pour in the booze, season well then remove the pan from the heat and leave to cool. Mix the onion-bacon mixture with all the remaining ingredients until they are a stuffing consistency.

SIMPLE SAUSAGEMEAT

1 garlic clove
100ml cold water
1 medium onion
15g butter
1 apple, peeled and cored
100g fresh breadcrumbs
1kg pork sausage meat
1 small bunch parsley, leaves picked
a few sage leaves
salt and pepper

Crush the garlic to a paste with a little salt and stir the paste into the cold water. Purée the onion in a food processor. Melt the butter in a frying pan and fry the puréed onion until tender.

Grate the apple in the food processor, then change back to the regular blade and add the breadcrumbs, sausage meat and herbs. Switch to a high speed and, as the motor runs, pour the garlic flavoured water into the meat mixture. Season with pepper.

APPLE, SAGE AND CHESTNUT

20g butter
2 onions, diced
300g chestnuts, finely chopped
10 sage leaves, torn, plus a few to garnish
100g fresh breadcrumbs
3 granny smith apples, grated
200g pork sausage meat
salt and pepper

Melt the butter in a pan and fry the onions over a medium heat until translucent. Add the chestnuts and sage and season well. Cook for 2 minutes, then remove from the heat.

In a large bowl, soak the breadcrumbs in 100ml water for a few minutes, until the water is all absorbed. Add the apples and sausage meat and beat well with a wooden spoon for about 3 minutes, to incorporate some air, which will expand during cooking and give you a fluffy rather than stodgy stuffing.

Cook as on page 164 and garnish with the remaining sage leaves before serving.

MIDDLE EASTERN STYLE

30g butter
2 shallots, diced
300g chicken, minced
6 sage leaves, chopped
4 apples, grated
10 dried apricots, soaked then finely chopped
100g toasted cashews
100g sultanas
2 tbsp mixture toasted cumin, cardamon and coriander
100g fresh breadcrumbs, soaked in a little milk
1 egg
50g butter
1 small bunch coriander, chopped
salt and pepper

Fry the shallots in the butter and season well (always use lots of seasoning in stuffings). Leave to cool, then combine with all the rest of the ingredients in a large bowl. Mix well and slap it around the bowl until you have a firm paste that smells fragrant.

PRUNE AND CHESTNUT

2 large shallots, diced
2 garlic cloves, crushed
60g butter
6 celery sticks, finely chopped
200g prunes in armagnac (below)
200ml port
100g cooked chestnuts, chopped
2 handfuls flat-leaf parsley, chopped
300g pork sausage meat
salt and pepper
PRUNES IN ARMAGNAC
200g agen prunes
2 earl grey teabags
juice and pared rind of 1 orange
100ml armagnac

Put the prunes in a saucepan, add the teabags, orange juice and rind and cover with boiling water. Leave to soak overnight. Drain, discarding the teabags and rind. Chop the prunes and pour over the booze.

Sweat the shallots and garlic in the butter and season. Add the celery and chestnuts, raise the heat and cook for 2 minutes. Mix with the rest of the ingredients.

ROAST GROUSE WITH MADEIRA SAUCE

SERVES

4 grouse
4 garlic cloves
4 sage leaves
some olive oil
salt and pepper
4 handfuls watercress, to serve

SAUCE
125g grouse wings, neck and
   giblets, chopped
1 shallot, chopped
6 mushrooms, chopped
1 carrot, chopped
1 celery stalk, chopped
1 garlic clove, chopped
1 glass madeira
200ml chicken stock (page 20)
200ml meat stock, preferably
   veal stock
2 sage leaves

Ask your butcher to take the wings and neck off the birds so they are oven-ready, and give you the trimmings and giblets to take home.

Start with the sauce – it can be made the day before serving if preferred. In a wide pan, fry the wings and necks in a bit of oil until golden brown. Drain off the excess fat, add the chopped veg and garlic, and cook for 1 minute. Add the madeira, bring to the boil and reduce to a syrupy consistency. Add the chicken stock and boil until reduced by half, then add the meat stock and reduce again until you have a light sauce.

When the sauce is nearly ready, chop the giblets, season them and add to the sauce to enrich it. Bring the sauce to the boil once more and pass through a fine sieve. Sit the sage leaves in the sauce to add flavour. Keep it warm until serving, or allow to cool if making in advance.

To cook the grouse, heat the oven to 200°C (gas 6) and put a roasting tray in it to get hot as well. Place one garlic clove and a sage leaf in each bird then season inside and out. Heat a large frying pan with a little oil over a high heat and seal the birds all over until golden.

Put the birds in the roasting tray with a little olive oil and roast for 8 minutes, basting frequently. Remove from the oven and let rest for a minute. Reheat the sauce if necessary and serve with the grouse.

GAME CHIPS

4 large potatoes
2 litres vegetable oil
salt

To make these at home it is helpful to have a mandoline or a mandoline-style slicing attachment for your food processor. You only need a few game chips for each serving; the trouble is that once you start cooking them they quickly disappear.

Slice the potatoes very thinly – so thin that if held up to the light it will shine through. Fill a sink or bowl with cold water and wash the sliced potatoes. Change the water and repeat until the water stays clear, indicating that most of the starch has been removed.

Heat the oil to 190°C in a deep-fryer. Working in batches of 100g, gently place each potato slice in the oil as if you were the dealer at a card game. After 3 minutes frying, stir well so that they do not stick together (if they are sticking, the oil may not be hot enough or the potato has not been thoroughly washed of starch). Continue frying and stirring the chips for 8 to 10 minutes.

Remove the chips from the oil and drain well on kitchen paper. Repeat with the remaining potatoes. Place the chips in a brown paper bag while still warm and sprinkle with salt.

PHEASANT WRAPPED IN PROSCIUTTO WITH POLENTA

SERVES 🐓🐓🐓🐓

8 slices parma ham
16 sage leaves
8 pheasant breasts, trimmed of
   excess fat
100g butter
40ml olive oil
juice of 1 large lemon
flaky sea salt and pepper

POLENTA
300ml milk
1 garlic clove, crushed
¼ tsp salt
½ tsp ground black pepper
100g instant polenta
120ml double cream
30g parmesan cheese, grated
70g mascarpone

Lay two slices of ham side-by-side and slightly overlapping, and place a sage leaf in the middle. Lay a pheasant breast on top, skin-side down. Season well and place a couple of sage leaves on the flesh side, then add a good knob of butter. Lay the other breast on top skin-side up to make a sandwich. Place another sage leaf on top of that breast and carefully fold the ham over the breasts, wrapping tightly. Repeat with the remaining ham and pheasant. This operation can be done the day before serving and in fact the sage flavours the meat a little more when left for some time.

To make the polenta, put 200ml water in a saucepan with the milk, garlic, salt and pepper, and bring to a rolling boil. Add the polenta, stirring constantly in a clockwise direction, and keep stirring until the mixture thickens and comes back to the boil. Reduce the heat to very low and cook, stirring very frequently, for 45 minutes. Add the cream and parmesan cheese, and continue cooking over a low heat for another 10 minutes, until the cheese has completely dissolved. Remove the pan from the heat and stir the mascarpone into the polenta. Leave to cool for 10 minutes before serving.

Meanwhile, heat the oven to 200°C (gas 6). Heat a heavy frying pan over a high heat. Pour a little oil into the hot pan and add the breasts carefully so as not to splash yourself. Leave to cook for 3 minutes, until the edges start to brown, then turn over and cook for a further 3 minutes. Transfer the pheasant to a baking dish and place in the oven for 8 minutes, watching so they don't stick or get too brown.

Set the pheasant aside and put the baking dish with pan juices over a low heat. Stir in the remaining butter and lemon juice to make a sauce. Serve the pheasant with the polenta and sauce.

ROAST PARTRIDGE WITH POTATOES AND ROSEMARY

SERVES

200g butter
2kg large potatoes, peeled and thinly sliced
300g white onions, sliced
200ml strong chicken or game stock (pages 20-21)
8 partridges
1 large handful sage
10 rosemary branches
salt and pepper

Boulanger potatoes with lashings of rosemary and the juices of roast partridges dripping into them – yum!

Heat the oven to 180°C (gas 4). Grease a large ovenproof dish with plenty of butter. Mix the sliced potatoes and onions with a good amount of salt and pepper then add the stock. Pour the lot into the greased dish and pat it all down. Bake for 40 minutes.

Meanwhile, rub the birds with some more of the butter, season well and stuff the cavities with sage. Rub the rosemary branches with oil and salt.

When the potatoes have been cooking for 40 minutes, raise the heat to 200°C (gas 6) and lay half the rosemary on the potatoes. Sit the birds on top and cover with the rest of the rosemary. Shut the oven door and do not open it for 20 minutes.

Take the potatoes and partridges from the oven and serve – you can't eat the rosemary but it smells so beautiful, just take the dish to the table and listen to the gushing enthusiasm.

FIVE-SPICED CHINESE DUCK WITH BOK CHOY AND OYSTER SAUCE

SERVES

DUCK
1 large Chinese duck
150g sugar
1 pinch sea salt
6 star anise
12cm piece root ginger, peeled
   and sliced
1 small bunch spring onions,
   roughly chopped
2 tbsp maltose
2½ tbsp red wine vinegar

BOK CHOY
60ml fish sauce
400g bok choy, halved
   lengthways
50ml oyster sauce
1 long red chilli, thinly sliced
   at an angle
coriander leaves, to garnish

Chinese or Peking ducks, as they are often called in supermarkets, are bred with less fat than other ducks, so the skin crisps up much better. I usually roast two ducks at a time and then freeze one for another day.

Two days before serving, wash the duck inside and out with cold water, then drain and pat dry. Mix together the sugar, salt, star anise, ginger and spring onions. Fill the cavity with this, then secure it with a wooden skewer, soaked in water.

Put a kettle of water on to boil. Mix the maltose and 2 tablespoons of the vinegar with a tablespoon of the boiling water and set aside. Put the remaining boiled water in a jug, add the last ½ tablespoon of vinegar and pour over the duck. The boiling water opens up the pores, while the vinegar helps strip some of the waxiness from the skin, so it will be more receptive to the maltose. Smear the maltose mixture over the duck and hang it up to dry overnight.

Heat the oven to 220°C (gas 7). Put a little water in the bottom of a roasting tin, and put the duck on a rack over the top. Roast for about 45 minutes, then carefully take the duck off the rack and drain off the water and fat. Return the duck to the rack and continue roasting for another 40 minutes or until the duck is well done – there is no such thing as rare Chinese roast duck! Take the duck from the oven and let it sit for a good 20 minutes. (You can let it cool completely, then wrap and freeze at this point).

Take the meat off the bone. Put the bones in a pot with 1 litre water and the fish sauce. Bring to the boil and simmer for 5 minutes. Add the bok choy and cook for 1 to 2 minutes, then lift them out.

Divide the bok choy among four serving bowls. Swirl some oyster sauce around. Cut the duck up so that each person gets some leg and breast meat on top of the vegetables. Sprinkle with chilli, spoon over a little of the broth and garnish with coriander leaves.

Tip: I am a great believer in intensifying flavour any way you can, so before roasting Chinese ducks I often put some sugar, spices and spring onions inside, which adds enormously to the flavour and also helps tenderize the meat.

GOOSE AND MUSTARD FRUITS WITH MARSALA SAUCE

SERVES

3.5kg goose
1 head garlic
3 thyme sprigs
3 rosemary sprigs
2 onions, halved but unpeeled
6 rashers smoked streaky
  bacon
mostarda di Cremona, to serve
salt and pepper

MARSALA SAUCE
2 shallots, chopped
12 juniper berries, crushed
a little olive oil
100ml brandy
150ml marsala
150ml madeira
200ml your choice of poultry
  or meat stock

I like my roast goose to be almost falling off the bone. The meat can be used cold the next day in a salad.

You can do this on the day of cooking, but I prefer to do it the day before: clean the goose inside and out, trim off any excess fat and season inside and out. Put the garlic, thyme and rosemary in the cavity with 125ml water. Refrigerate until 2 hours before roasting.

Heat the oven to 220°C (gas 7). Set the goose on a wire rack in a roasting tin and pour in 375ml water. Place the unpeeled onion halves around the bird and lay the bacon over the breast. Cover the whole thing with foil, sealing it well, and roast for 1 hour.

Take the goose from the oven and remove the foil. (The bacon is delicious on fresh white buttered bread.) Reduce the oven to 200°C (gas 6) and cook uncovered for a further 1 hour, basting twice.

Meanwhile, start the sauce. Sweat the shallots and juniper berries in a little oil until soft. Add all the alcohol and flame carefully. Pour in the stock, bring to the boil and reduce to a sauce consistency. Strain and set aside.

When the goose is cooked, put it aside to rest for 15 minutes. Drain the pan juices from the roasting tray and set aside. Put the roasting tin on the stove-top and lay the onions in it cut-side down for a few minutes so they soak up the flavours.

When the pan juices have separated, skim off and discard the fat. Open the goose slightly and drain the liquid. Add this, the remaining pan juices and the marsala sauce to the roasting tin and bring to the boil. When the sauce starts to thicken, strain it and season to taste.

Return the bird to the oven for 15 minutes to crisp up, then serve with the marsala sauce and mostarda.

GUINEA FOWL WITH SWEET POTATOES

SERVES

100g butter, plus 1 knob extra
1 tsp smoked paprika
2 large sweet potatoes
1 large guinea fowl, over 1kg
juice of 1 lemon, plus the
    remains chopped
1 onion, chopped
4 black peppercorns, crushed
1 rosemary branch
20ml olive oil
4 banana shallots, peeled and
    quartered lengthways
about 250ml yoghurt
1 tsp sumac (optional)
toasted flatbreads, to serve
salt and pepper

Mix the butter and smoked paprika together. Peel the sweet potatoes and halve each one lengthways down the centre, then cut each half into four hunks.

Heat the oven to 200°C (gas 6). Remove the innards from the guinea fowl, wash it well inside and dry. Fill the cavity with the chopped lemon and onion, crushed peppercorns, some salt and the rosemary. Season the outside of the bird with salt and pepper, then brush the flavoured butter all over the front and legs.

Put a large ovenproof pan or roasting dish over a high heat. Add a knob of butter with the oil and, once sizzling, cook the sweet potatoes and shallots for 5 minutes. Put the bird in, give the pan a good shake, then transfer to the oven and roast for 1 hour, basting frequently.

Remove from the oven and allow the bird to rest for 5 minutes before carving. Stir the lemon juice into the yoghurt, place in a serving bowl and sprinkle with the sumac. Serve the chicken with the yoghurt and toasted flatbreads, and the pan juices as gravy.

If you have not worked it out yet then I am about to tell you: I am actually quite a lazy cook. Well, not really lazy, but I don't believe in being a slave to the kitchen. Entertaining, feeding the family and eating well are all things I love to do but I don't feel I have to spend days and days in the kitchen to get a great result.

The one pot wonder is an antidote for the busy person who loves to cook but has guilt trips about eating good food if time is limited. I say plonk it all in. Make sure you are careful and gentle and use great produce, but put it in the pot and walk away and do whatever else needs to be done.

One pot wonders are meant to be a centrepiece that everyone dives into, taking the bits they like and leaving the bits they don't, sharing great food and great conversation. Honestly, this is one of the most enjoyable ways to cook. Take your time with the shopping and then, when you get home, wiz-bang: it's dinner, lunch or even brunch without much effort.

one pot wonders

HEARTY CHICKEN CASSEROLE
WITH DUMPLINGS

SERVES 🐔 🐔 🐔 🐔 🐔 🐔

6 chicken breasts, bone in,
   each cut into 3 pieces
3 tbsp plain flour
100ml vegetable oil
350g button onions, peeled, or
   4 medium onions, peeled
   and cut into 8
200g smoked bacon
3 garlic cloves, crushed
300g flat mushrooms, sliced
3 large carrots, peeled and cut
   into hunks
2 large potatoes, peeled and
   diced
2 bay leaves
2 tbsp redcurrant jelly
375ml red wine
300ml chicken stock (page 20)
salt and pepper

DUMPLINGS
150g suet
350g self raising flour
150ml warm water

Heat the oven to 200°C (gas 6). Put the flour in a plastic bag and season with lots of salt and pepper. Drop the chicken into the flour and shake like mad to coat well.

Heat the oil in a large casserole and brown the chicken pieces over a high heat. Remove the chicken and reduce the heat. Add the onions and bacon and cook for 5 to 8 minutes until they are coloured and smell good. Add the garlic, then the mushies, carrots, potatoes, bay leaves and redcurrant jelly. Stir well. Put the chook back in and stir to coat well. Pour in the wine and stock. Cover and bring to the boil then transfer the pot to the oven for 40 minutes.

To make the dumplings, combine the suet, flour and a big pinch of salt in a mixing bowl. Gradually stir in the warm water, mixing to give a heavy dough. Roll the mixture into balls about the size of a golf ball. Take the casserole from the oven, drop the dumplings into it and return to the oven for a final 20 minutes, until the dumplings are cooked.

COQ AU VIN

SERVES 🐔🐔🐔🐔🐔🐔🐔🐔🐔🐔

2 large chickens, each cut into
  8, or 16 pieces of chicken
about 100g butter
24 small shallots, peeled
10 rashers smoked bacon or
  200g pancetta, cubed
3 garlic cloves, squashed
750ml full-bodied red wine
200g button mushrooms,
  sliced
1 large handful chopped
  parsley
salt and pepper

Elizabeth David cooked her chicken whole, then caramelized onions in butter and sugar and added them to the casserole at the end of cooking. Other people prefer to joint their fowl and add mushrooms for the last few minutes. Some people reckon you should use a tough boiling fowl, others a plumper bird. What do I think? It is important to use a chicken with quite a bit of fat in it, not a scrawny thing, and don't kill the texture by overcooking. This is a two-chook recipe for eight or ten people, if you are cooking for less halve it.

Heat the oven to 200°C (gas 6). Season the chicken pieces generously. Heat 50g of the butter in a casserole and fry the chicken with half the shallots and half the bacon. When everything is coloured, add the garlic and wine. Bring to the boil, then cover tightly and transfer to the oven for 1 to 1½ hours, until the chicken is cooked through.

In a frying pan, cook the remaining shallots with 50g butter and a small glass of water. When the water has evaporated the onions will be soft. Add the rest of the bacon and the mushrooms, plus some more butter if needed. Season with lots of ground pepper and a little salt. Toss until the bacon and mushrooms are just golden, then tip them into the casserole. Add loads of chopped parsley and serve.

POT AU FEU

SERVES

1 very large chicken, about 2.5kg
375ml white wine
4 large banana shallots
1 bouquet garni made with
  3 bay leaves, 3 thyme sprigs,
  2 celery sticks and 3 cloves
4 carrots, peeled and chopped
2 leeks, chopped
20 new potatoes, peeled
1 small celeriac, peeled and
  chopped

DUMPLINGS
150g suet
350g self-raising flour
1 large handful chopped parsley
150ml warm water

STUFFING
200g sausagemeat
100g thick-cut bacon, diced
3 or 4 chicken livers, chopped
  (optional)
3 sage leaves, chopped
1 egg
2 garlic cloves, chopped
4 banana shallots, diced
1 bunch flat-leaf parsley,
  chopped
2 large handfuls fresh
  breadcrumbs
salt and pepper

Heat the oven to 190°C (gas 5). To make the stuffing, put all the ingredients in a bowl and mix to a paste.

You'll need a cast-iron casserole dish large enough to fit the bird. Trim the chicken cavity of any excess fat and fill with the stuffing, making sure that you close each end with a couple of big skewers and then cut off the ends so it all fits in the pot. Put the chicken in the casserole. Add the wine, shallots, bouquet garni and some salt and pepper. Pour in enough water to rise one knuckle above the bird, then cover and place in the oven for 1½ hours.

To make the dumplings, mix the suet, flour, parsley and a big pinch of salt in a large bowl and stir in the warm water to make a heavy dough. Roll the mixture into balls the size of a golfball.

Take the casserole from the oven and add the carrots, leeks, potatoes and celeriac, being careful not to move the chicken too much. Return to the oven for half an hour.

Remove the pot from the oven again. Lift out the chicken, put it on a plate, cover tightly with cling film and set aside. Leave all the veg in the pot and add the dumplings. Bring the pot to the boil then reduce to a simmer and cook for 15 minutes.

Test the veg and, if they are cooked, take the skin off the chook and discard it. Cut up the meat and the stuffing and keep them warm. Heat your serving bowls and divide the chicken, stuffing, vegetables and dumplings between them. Cover with the pan juices and serve with mustard and crusty bread.

BRAISED GUINEA FOWL WITH CELERIAC AND CRISP BACON

SERVES

300g bacon or pancetta, cut
  into thick chunks
2 guinea fowl, each cut into
  8 pieces
100g plain flour
2 onions, sliced
1 lemon, halved
2 bay leaves
1 handful dried mushrooms
10 garlic cloves
400ml chicken stock (page 20)
50ml white or red wine vinegar
500g celeriac, peeled and cut
  into hunks the same size as
  the guinea fowl
1 small bunch coriander,
  picked
1 bunch tarragon, chopped
salt and pepper

The idea is that the birds are cooked in the bacon fat and the bacon is saved to be scattered on top. For this you will need thick fatty bacon, maybe even pancetta lardons, which you can get at a supermarket.

Heat the oven to 180ºC (gas 4). Drop the bacon into a large cold cast-iron casserole and set it over a high heat. As it heats, the fat will melt and the bacon will fry in its own fat. Once coloured and crisp, add a good amount of salt and pepper, reduce the heat and set the bacon aside on kitchen paper.

Dust the guinea fowl pieces in the flour then, working in batches, add them to the casserole and colour in the bacon fat. Add the onions, lemon, bay leaves, dried mushrooms and garlic to the guinea fowl and let them colour for a few minutes. Add the stock, vinegar and celeriac and bring to the boil, giving the casserole a bloody good stir.

Pop it all in the oven to cook uncovered for 45 minutes. Just before serving, heat the bacon in a frying pan and scatter over the casserole along with the coriander and tarragon. Serve with a good blob of mustard.

GUINEA FOWL TAGINE

SERVES

1 guinea fowl
a little olive oil
2 carrots, cut into chunks
2 red onions, cut into chunks
6 dried prunes, dates or figs
rind of 1 preserved lemon, cut
   into strips
1 mint sprig, leaves chopped
harissa, to serve

CHERMOULA
1 large red onion, roughly
   chopped
1 large garlic clove
1.5cm piece ginger, roughly
   chopped
100ml olive oil
100ml lemon juice
$^1/_2$ tsp Thai fish sauce
1 heaped tsp honey
$^1/_2$ tsp ground cumin
$^1/_2$ tsp ground paprika
$^1/_2$ tsp turmeric powder
$^1/_2$ tsp hot chilli powder
1 handful flat-leaf parsley
1 handful coriander

COUSCOUS
100g couscous
1 tsp salt
100g butter, cubed
1 small handful sultanas

I really hope that no one who tries this dish portions it up neatly in the kitchen and then takes it to the table, or packs the couscous into little ring moulds and serves slivers of guinea fowl balanced on top. This is wonderful, honest, stick-the-pot-in-the-middle-of-the-table food.

The day before cooking, put all the ingredients for the chermoula in a blender and process until smooth. Pour over the bird and marinate in the fridge overnight.

Next day, heat the oven to 220°C (gas 7). Heat a little olive oil in a large frying pan and brown the bird on all sides over a high heat. Put the carrots, onions and fruit into the tagine and place the guinea fowl on top. Pour in about 400ml water – enough to come 1cm from the top of the tagine base. Cover and cook in the oven for about 45 minutes, then turn the heat down to 180°C (gas 4) and cook for another 45 minutes.

About 15 minutes before serving, rinse the couscous in cold water and put in a shallow bowl. Season with salt and scatter with the butter and sultanas. Pour on enough boiling water to cover the couscous by about 1cm. Cover and leave for 10 minutes or until the grains are plump and tender.

Open the tagine at the table and scatter with the preserved lemon and mint. Serve the couscous and harissa separately.

Variation: you can use this recipe for whole chicken, or lamb shanks, but increase the cooking time to 3 hours. For pigeons, reduce it to 1 hour. In each case, lower the temperature halfway through cooking time.

PIGEONS IN A POT

SERVES

olive oil
4 pigeons
200g smoked bacon or
   pancetta, cut into pieces
50g dried ceps
1 cabbage, cut into chunks
18 sage leaves
100g butter
squeeze of lemon juice
salt and pepper

Unlike most game, pigeon is only hung briefly; otherwise the bird takes on a sour taste. If you can, buy French pigeons that have been grain fed; they are more expensive, but worth it for the superb quality.

Heat the oven to 220°C (gas 7). Heat the oil in a large casserole. Season the pigeons, put them into the pan and cook until browned, then remove and keep warm. Add a little more oil to the pan and, when hot, add the bacon or pancetta, dried ceps, cabbage and about two-thirds of the sage. Toss until the pancetta and vegetables colour.

Sit the pigeons back on top of the bacon, ceps and cabbage. Add the butter then cover the pot and transfer to the oven for about 30 minutes, until the breast meat is pink but the leg meat is done to the point where it comes easily from the bone.

Squeeze the lemon juice over the top and throw on the rest of the sage. This is fab with boiled potatoes and mustard.

DUCK WITH OLIVES AND VINEGAR SAUCE

SERVES

1 whole duck, cut into 8 pieces
3 tbsp plain flour
1 tsp flaky sea salt
½ tsp white pepper
100ml olive oil
20g butter
100ml cabernet sauvignon
   vinegar
30ml white wine
150g pitted black olives
4 shallots, roughly chopped
1 garlic clove, chopped
3 bay leaves
2 rosemary branches, leaves
   picked

Make sure you use a good smooth-tasting cabernet sauvignon vinegar for this. If you want to use sherry vinegar, or your vinegar tastes sharp, reduce the volume to 50ml. Keep your malt vinegar for your chips.

Heat the oven to 160°C (gas 3). Season the flour with sea salt and white pepper and dust the duck pieces in it. Heat a small amount of the olive oil in a casserole with the butter and brown the duck. Add the remaining olive oil, vinegar, wine, olives, shallots, garlic and bay leaves. Give the pan a good shuffle and leave on the stove for 5 to 8 minutes to give the shallots some colour.

Add the rosemary, then cover and transfer the casserole to the oven for 1 hour 20 minutes. Serve with great mashed potatoes (page 157).

SLOW ROAST PHEASANTS
BARLEY AND WILD MUSHROOMS

SERVES

180g butter
60ml vegetable oil
2 large pheasants
200g wild mushrooms
4 large flat mushrooms,
    chopped roughly
3 large onions, quartered
200g pearl barley
1.5 litres chicken or game stock
    (pages 20-21)
100g picked watercress
salt and pepper

'Slowly slowly' they say with barley and this meaty little number needs time in the oven. It will be soft and delicious, with the breasts still moist – a revelation with pheasant.

Heat the oven to 160°C (gas 3). Melt 100g of butter with the oil in a casserole. Season the birds, brown them all over and remove from the pot. Fry the wild mushrooms in the pan juices, then lift them out. Put the chopped field mushrooms and onions in the casserole and fry them well. Stir in the barley.

Return the birds to the pot and push them in well so they sink into the barley. Sprinkle the wild mushrooms over then pour in the stock and bring to the boil. Cover and place in the oven for at least 1 hour.

Take the casserole from the oven and test the barley is done. Take the birds out and set aside. Give the barley a good stir, add the remaining 80g butter then taste and season as necessary.

Break the birds up using your hands and/or a knife and fork – they should come apart easily. Serve the pheasant on the barley, scattered with watercress.

I am going to be controversial: the Australians make the best pies in the world. Sorry, but it is true. When I say pie, I mean the sort you hold in your hands and let the filling dribble down your chin and between your fingers. So, as an Australian, I am proud to present you with a few inspiring pies and tarts, the later being posher pies without a lid.

Some of my all-time favourites, which I am very proud of and that many believe to be naff, are also in here, such as the curry puff made with leftover chicken or turkey. We always had them on Boxing Day and Easter Monday (it just goes to show how expensive chicken was when I was a kid, we only had it on special occasions). I've also included that other 1970s favourite (think Abigail's Party): the vol au vent.

The pies in this chapter vary from classics such as chicken and leek and the best-ever game pie with raised water pastry, to the great American-inspired chicken pot pie. All these recipes are meant to inspire. Who ate all the pies? I did, and loved every single one.

tarts, pies & pastries

CHICKEN POT PIE

SERVES

750g chicken thigh and breast
   fillets, halved
250ml chicken stock (page 20)
125ml single cream or creamy
   milk
6 celery stalks, chopped
2 leeks, cut into 1cm pieces
250g new potatoes, halved
   crossways
4 garlic cloves, chopped
500g cooked gammon or ham,
   cut into 2.5 cm cubes
50g butter
6 tbsp plain flour
½ tsp freshly grated nutmeg
4 tbsp chopped flat-leaf
   parsley
375g ready-made puff pastry
1 egg yolk beaten with 1 tbsp
   milk, for glazing
salt and pepper

Put the chicken, stock, cream, celery, leeks, potatoes, garlic and gammon in a large saucepan. Bring to the boil then reduce the heat, cover and simmer for 20 to 25 minutes or until the chicken is tender.

Set a colander over a large heatproof measuring jug and pour the contents of the pan into it: you need 500ml of liquid, so discard any extra or make up the quantity using extra cream or milk.

Clean and dry the pan. Add the butter and melt over a moderate heat. Stir in the flour until bubbling, but do not let the mixture colour. Add the reserved liquid, about a third at a time, stirring well so that the mixture is thick, smooth and velvety. Stir in the nutmeg and parsley, then season to taste. Add the contents of the colander and toss gently in the sauce until well coated. Let cool for 10 minutes. (You can make the filling in advance up to this point and store it in the fridge.)

Heat the oven to 200°C (gas 6). Take a 1.2 litre pie dish 7.5cm deep and roll out the pastry so that it is 5mm thick and a bit bigger than the pie dish. Put the pie dish upside down on the pastry and cut around it, leaving a 3cm border. Ladle the filling into the dish, piling it up high in the centre.

Set the pastry lid on top and press into place, trimming off any excess. Cut a little vent in the centre, then brush the egg glaze over the pastry. At this point you can mark decorative patterns in the pastry, if liked, or leave it plain.

Bake towards the top of the oven for 25 minutes or until the pastry has puffed, then reduce the temperature to 180°C (gas 4) and cook for a further 15 minutes or until the pastry is crusty and golden. (If you made the filling in advance and it was cold when you put it in the oven, continue cooking for a further 30 minutes). If the pastry browns too quickly, cover it with a folded sheet of damp parchment. Serve hot, straight from the dish.

CHICKEN, LEEK AND MUSHROOM PIE

SERVES

100g butter
2 leeks, cut into 1cm pieces
6 celery stalks, chopped
50g plain flour, plus 6 tbsp
extra
250ml chicken stock (page 20)
125ml single cream
200g button mushrooms
750g roast chicken meat,
without skin or bone
4 tbsp chopped flat-leaf
parsley
375g ready-made puff pastry
1 egg yolk beaten with 1 tbsp
milk, for glazing
salt and pepper

Melt 50g butter in a large saucepan, add the leeks and celery and cook for 5 minutes stirring constantly. Add 50g flour and mix to a paste. Stir in the stock and cream. Bring to the boil, reduce the heat, cover and simmer for 15 minutes. Remove from the heat and add the mushrooms and chicken. Season and add the parsley

Heat the oven to 220°C (gas 7). Take a 1.2 litre pie dish 7.5cm deep and roll out the pastry so that it is 5mm thick and at least 5cm bigger than the pie dish. Put the pie dish upside down on the pastry and cut around it, leaving a 3cm border. Cut a 2cm-wide strip of pastry to fit around the edge of the dish. Brush the edge with water and stick the strip on top. Ladle the filling into the dish, piling it up high in the centre.

Wet the pastry strip. Set the pastry lid on top and press into place, trimming off any excess. Cut a small vent in the centre then brush the pastry with the egg glaze. Mark decorative patterns in the pastry or leave plain as preferred.

Bake towards the top of the oven for 25 minutes, then reduce to 200°C (gas 6) and cook for a further 15 minutes or until the pastry is crusty and golden. If the pastry browns too quickly, cover it with a folded sheet of damp baking parchment. Serve hot, straight from the dish.

RAISED CHICKEN AND PARTRIDGE PIE

SERVES

FILLING

1kg chicken, boned, skinned and cut into thumb-sized chunks (keep all the trimmings)
8 partridge breasts
500g pork shoulder, boned, skinned and casually minced (keep all the trimmings)
1 bay leaf
2 tsp salt
2 tsp cayenne pepper
1 tsp ground white pepper
1 tsp ground black pepper
60ml sherry
3 hard-boiled eggs, yolks only
1 tsp gelatine powder

CRUST

75g lard
300g plain flour
1 tsp salt
1 egg, beaten, for glazing

This cold pie is an opportunity for the cook to show off! You will need a beautiful fluted oval mould.

First take all the poultry and pork trimmings and put them in a large saucepan with the bay leaf. Cover with water, bring to the boil and simmer for 3 hours while you get on with making the pie.

Combine the salt and spices in a bowl, add the sherry and stir to dissolve. Mix the poultry and pork together on a work surface, then push the mixture out flat. Pour over the spiced sherry and roll it all together, mixing well.

To make the crust, put the lard in a saucepan with 70ml water and bring to the boil. Sift the flour and salt together twice into a large bowl. Add the hot liquid and stir like mad until combined. Keep the pastry covered and work with it while still warm.

Heat the oven to 180°C (gas 4). Take three-quarters of the pastry, roll it out to 1cm thick and line the mould. Trim away the excess. Fill halfway with the meat mixture. Make three indentations down the middle of it and insert the egg yolks. Top with the rest of the meat, piling it a little beyond the top of the mould.

Roll out the remaining pastry to make the lid. Rub the rim of the pie with water and press on the lid. Crimp the edges so the pie is well sealed. Brush with egg and decorate with flowers or leaves made with the pastry trimmings. Cut a vent in the centre of the lid.

Bake for 30 minutes, then reduce the oven temperature to 150°C (gas 2) and continue baking for 2 hours. Remove the pie from the oven and leave to cool completely.

Meanwhile, strain the stock and measure 200ml into a jug. Stir in the gelatine and season well. When the pie is at room temperature, use a funnel to pour the stock into the pie through the vent. Chill for at least 2 hours, preferably overnight, before serving.

GOOD OLD CHICKEN OR TURKEY VOL AU VENTS

MAKES

375g ready-made puff pastry
1 egg beaten with a little milk
50g button mushrooms, sliced
10g butter, plus extra for
  greasing
300g cooked chicken or turkey
  meat
200ml thick béchamel sauce
225g dry breadcrumbs
salt and pepper

A throwback to the 1970s, this is a real classy way to use up leftovers. I love vol au vents of thick creamy mushroom sauce with bits of chicken or turkey. You can buy the vol au vent cases or make them yourself.

Heat the oven to 200°C (gas 6). Roll out the pastry and use a cutter or glass to cut it into 24 discs. Place half the discs on a greased baking tray and brush them with the egg wash. Using a smaller cutter than the first, cut holes from the centre of the remaining pastry discs so that you have 12 rings. Lay the rings on top of the discs on the tray. Use a fork to prick holes in the base of the vol au vents.

Bake for 20 minutes or until golden and risen but not crisp. You should be able to easily push down the centres of the vol au vents so they can take the filling.

Meanwhile, gently fry the mushrooms in the butter and season well. Remove from the heat. Stir in the chicken or turkey, then pour over the béchamel and mix well. Spoon some filling into each vol au vent, then sprinkle over the breadcrumbs and put the little wonders back into the oven for 15 minutes.

CURRY PUFFS

MAKES

200g cooked chicken or turkey,
   shredded
100ml thick curry sauce
   (bought is fine)
50g frozen peas, defrosted
375g ready-made puff pastry
milk, for glazing
butter, for greasing

These are one of the best ways to use up leftover turkey or chicken and should be quite small – two bites is enough.

Mix the chicken or turkey, curry sauce and peas together and set aside.

Roll out the pastry to about 5mm thick and cut into 20 rounds the size of a scone. Brush the discs lightly with milk. Put a heaped teaspoon of curry mixture in the middle of each disc and fold into a crescent shape. Pick each one up and push the edges together to seal well.

Place the puffs on a greased baking tray and when they are all filled and lined up like soldiers, brush each one with more milk. Put them in the fridge to chill before they go in the oven – they can sit there for up to a day.

When ready to cook, heat the oven to 200°C (gas 6) and bake the curry puffs for 25 to 30 minutes. Serve hot.

TURKEY AND POTATO PASTIES

SERVES 🐔 🐔 🐔 🐔

50g butter
1 large onion, sliced
1 large potato, peeled and
 thinly sliced
300g turkey meat, roughly
 chopped
50ml soured cream
375g ready-made puff pastry
milk, for brushing
salt and pepper

Melt the butter in a saucepan. Add the onion and let it soften. Season really well, adding loads of pepper. Add the potato and cook for just 3 or 4 minutes more. Transfer the onion and potato to a mixing bowl. Mix in the turkey and soured cream, then chill.

Roll out the pastry to about 5mm thick and cut into four rounds using a small plate as a guide. Divide the filling among the pastry rounds. Brush the edges with milk then fold and seal the edges well. Place on a baking sheet and chill for 30 minutes – in the freezer if possible.

Heat the oven to 200°C (gas 6) and bake the pasties for 40 minutes. Serve immediately or cool and eat cold if you are a weirdy English person.

PARTRIDGE PITHIVIER
WITH CEPS AND RED WINE

MAKES

375g ready-made puff pastry
3 large roast partridges
50g butter, plus extra for
  greasing
1 shallot, diced
100g wild mushrooms
1 large handful chives,
  chopped
1 handful chopped parsley
milk, for glazing
salt and pepper

SAUCE
50g dried ceps, soaked in
  warm water for 30 minutes
50g butter
2 shallots, sliced
100ml port
200ml red wine
100ml stock

This is the poshest of pies. A pithivier is shaped like a Catherine wheel – a dome with spiral marks on top. Roast the partridges in advance – they'll need about 15 minutes in the oven.

Roll out the pastry to 5mm thick. Cut into twelve discs about the size of a coffee cup and chill until needed.

Strip the roasted birds of their meat and shred it. Melt the butter in a saucepan, add the shallots and cook until softened, then add the mushrooms and cook for another minute or so. Season to taste, mix in the partridge meat and herbs, and set aside to cool.

To make the pies, arrange six of the pastry discs evenly spaced on a greased baking sheet. Pile a good amount of the partridge filling in the centre of each, but leave a decent rim of pastry at the edge. Brush these edges with milk and lay the remaining pastry discs on top. Press down to give little mounds and seal the edges with a fork.

Use a blunt knife to score the pastry from the centre top to the bottom in a semi-circle and repeat, working your way around each pithivier to make a wheel pattern. Brush the pastries with milk and chill for at least 10 minutes and up to 24 hours if need be.

When ready to cook, heat the oven to 200°C (gas 6) and bake the pithivier for 30 minutes or until well browned.

Meanwhile, make the sauce. Melt the butter in a saucepan and cook the shallots until soft. Drain the rehydrated mushrooms and add to the shallots. Season well and cook for 5 minutes until fragrant. Add the port, bring to the boil and reduce the volume of liquid by half. Add the wine and stock and return to the boil. When the sauce is thick and reduced to about 150ml, it is ready.

Spoon the sauce on serving plates and sit the posh little pies on top.

PASTILLA

SERVES 🐓🐓🐓🐓🐓🐓

4 legs confit duck (page 234),
   plus a little fat from the confit
1 onion, finely diced
1 cinnamon stick
1 handful parsley, coriander
   and thyme, tied together,
   plus 1 handful parsley and
   coriander, chopped
freshly ground black pepper
3 whole eggs, plus 2 yolks
2 tbsp icing sugar
1 tsp ground cinnamon
1 handful roast almonds
200g brik pastry (pâte brique),
   or filo pastry
20-50g butter, melted
a little vegetable oil (if using
   brik pastry)

**Many people make pastilla with pigeon but I prefer it
with duck. Brik pastry is the correct one to use and
can be bought ready-made from Moroccan shops,
some French delis and food halls. I sometimes use filo
instead, but do be careful using filo this way as the
pastilla can become greasy if you add too much butter.**

Take a large cast-iron pan and heat the fat in it. Add the onion
and fry gently until translucent. Add the cinnamon stick and
bundle of herbs, then the duck and give the pan a good shake.
Grind in some pepper. Cover with water, bring to a simmer and
cook for 20 minutes until the duck has warmed through. Using a
slotted spoon or scoop, take all the bits out of the water,
reserving the duck. Bring the liquid to the boil and reduce by half.

Beat the eggs and yolks together, then mix in three-quarters each
of the icing sugar and cinnamon powder. Pour this into the water,
turn the heat off and stir like mad until it thickens like custard.
Grind the almonds, add them to the custard and leave to cool.

Strip the duck, chuck away the skin and bone, and shred the
meat. Mix it with the chopped herbs. When the custard is cool,
fold the duck and herbs into it to give a mixture that is moist but
not wet.

Heat the oven to 200°C (gas 6). Brush six little non-stick pie
dishes or blini pans with the melted butter and lay in the pastry,
leaving enough overhanging that it can be folded to seal the
filling. If you are using brik, use two or three layers of pastry and
brush vegetable oil lightly between each one; for filo, use four
layers with the tiniest amount of melted butter between each.

Divide the filling among the pastillas, then fold the pastry over
and brush the tops with more butter. Bake for 30 minutes, then
remove from the oven and leave to cool a little before turning out.
Sprinkle with the remaining icing sugar and cinnamon and serve.

WILD MUSHROOM TART
WITH PEPPERED GROUSE

SERVES

2 grouse
about 50ml olive oil
1 large handful thyme sprigs
200g mixed wild mushrooms
1 large shallot, diced
1 garlic clove, crushed
50ml brandy
50g mascarpone
4 little shortcrust tart cases,
  baked blind
1 large handful chopped
  parsley
salt and pepper

This little tart is rich and homely. It could be served as a light lunch or the starting point to a hearty meal. There are varying degrees of wildness when it comes to grouse, but you want a strong, full-flavoured, delicious wild bird shot from the sky. Ask your game dealer for two well-hung oven-ready grouse.

Heat the oven to 200°C (gas 6). Rub the birds with oil and season well with salt and lots and lots of black pepper. Stuff the cavities with thyme. Place an ovenproof frying pan over a medium heat and, when the pan is hot, add a little oil. Add the grouse and let them brown, turning three times to get an even colour.

Transfer the pan of grouse to the oven and cook for 3 minutes. Give the pan a little shuffle, then cook for a few minutes more. The bird should be very pink at centre.

Meanwhile, clean and season the mushrooms. Remove the grouse to a plate and put the pan of cooking juices over a medium heat. Add the shallot and garlic and cook slowly for 5 minutes or so until soft. Add the mushrooms and cook for 5 minutes more.

Taste the mixture, season as necessary and remove the mushrooms from the pan. Increase the heat and, when the pan is very hot, add the brandy and flame it carefully. Drop the mushies back in the pan and add the mascarpone. Turn off the heat.

Pop the tart cases in the oven to heat through for 5 minutes. Carve the meat from the grouse and slice it, then mix with some of the parsley and any juices from the birds. Pile the mushroom mixture into the hot pastry cases, top with the grouse, sprinkle with the last of the parsley and serve.

Budgets are a concern for many families but budget does not have to mean cheap and nasty. I am inspired by the cuisines of Italy, China, Thailand and France because they have great dishes in which the central ingredient is not a lump of meat but a staple such as flour, rice, couscous or lentils. This is truly clever cooking, where flavour is paramount.

The secret to doing these types of dishes well is to keep them simple. Add too many ingredients to a risotto and it will just be confused. Put too many fillings or sauces with pasta and the plate will never be clean (the sign of great food is a clean plate, after all). The greatest cooks have the confidence to make dishes simple; with just a few ingredients they can make something stunning.

Preparation is seriously important here. Don't rush and don't skimp. Buy quality – it is not that expensive and wow, what a difference. Try and make your own stock (oh, I know what you're thinking, but maybe you did freeze some). Take time to nurture your dish, make it the most beautiful pot of rice or the best noodle dish on the street. That is how some vendors in Thailand make a living after all – so go on, give it a whirl.

pasta, noodles & grains

SPAGHETTI WITH CURRIED CHICKEN BALLS

SERVES

1 large onion, finely chopped
50ml vegetable oil
2 tbsp curry powder
50ml milk
100g fresh breadcrumbs
1kg chicken mince
1 handful chopped parsley, and
   some other herbs if you like
500g dried spaghetti
300ml double cream
salt and pepper

Put the onion, vegetable oil and curry powder in a large casserole with a good grind of pepper and some salt. Turn the heat to medium and slowly cook the onions until soft but not coloured. Remove from the heat and lift out the onions, leaving the oil in the casserole.

In a large bowl combine half the fried onion with the milk and breadcrumbs. Add the chicken mince, lots of salt and pepper and the parsley. Mix really well until it becomes a paste rather than lumpy. Roll into balls the size of a ping pong ball.

Put the casserole over a high heat and add the meatballs. Cook, turning, for a good 10 minutes, until well browned. Meanwhile, bring a pot of water to the boil and cook the spaghetti according to the packet instructions.

When the meatballs are browned, add the rest of the onion and the cream and bring to the boil. Taste and season if necessary. Cook for another 5 minutes then turn off the heat. Drain the pasta. I like to put the whole lot together but you may want to serve the meatballs and spaghetti separately, which of course is wrong!

PENNE WITH RAGOUT OF GAME, SAUSAGE AND RED WINE

SERVES 🐓🐓🐓🐓🐓🐓🐓🐓

1 large onion, sliced
50g butter
2 thyme sprigs
200g spicy pork sausages,
　thickly sliced
8 pheasant legs, or a mix of
　game pieces, about 1kg in
　total
100g seasoned flour
50ml olive oil
50g bacon, sliced
1 leek, chopped
4 tomatoes, chopped
300ml stock
300ml red wine
2 bay leaves
750g dried penne pasta

This is a great way to use up all the trimmings and bits of game that sit in the freezer.

Heat the oven to 160°C (gas 3). In a casserole, sweat the onion gently with the butter and thyme until soft but not coloured. Add the spicy sausage and cook until crisp. Lift the sausages and onions from the pot and set aside.

Toss the pheasant or whatever game you are using in the seasoned flour. Add the oil to the pot and fry the meat, giving it a good colour. Add the bacon, leek and tomatoes and fry with a bit of vigour, stirring to smash the tomatoes. Mix the remaining flour with the stock and red wine and pour into the casserole. Add the bay leaves, onion and sausages and bring to the boil. Cover and place in the oven for 2 hours.

Take the pot from the oven and carefully lift the game out. Strip the meat from the bones and mince it roughly with a chopping knife. Discard the game scraps and thyme sprigs. Stir the meat back into the ragout and keep warm.

Cook the pasta according to the packet instructions, then drain it and add to the ragout. Bring to a rapid boil before serving.

ORRECHETTI WITH PARTRIDGE

SERVES

4 crowns of partridge
60g butter
24 small button mushrooms
30g dried ceps, crushed
200ml chicken stock (page 20)
300ml double cream
500g orrechetti pasta
100ml whipped soured cream
1 large bunch chives, chopped
salt and pepper

Mushrooms, cream sauce and shredded partridge with soft pasta and loads of chives – fantastic.

Heat the oven to 200°C (gas 6). Rub the partridges with oil and seasoning, place in a cast-iron pot and roast for 12 minutes. Remove from the oven and set the partridge crowns aside, placing the pot with all those lovely juices over a medium heat.

Add the butter, button mushrooms and ceps and cook for a few minutes. Pour in the stock, bring to the boil and reduce until the mixture is almost syrupy. Add the double cream and bring to the boil, then season to taste. Meanwhile, shred the meat and cook the pasta according to the packet instructions.

Stir the partridge and orrechetti into the mushroom mixture and bring to the boil once more. Spoon into serving plates. Top each dish with a blob of soured cream and sprinkle with chives.

FRESH PASTA

MAKES 600G
500g 00 flour, plus extra for
    dusting
1 pinch salt
4 whole eggs plus 3 egg yolks,
    beaten
1 tbsp olive oil

'00' flour is best for pasta. Softer flours absorb too much liquid so the pasta won't be strong enough.

Put the flour and salt in a food processor. Add half the beaten eggs and mix until incorporated. Add the oil and whiz again.

Add the remaining eggs a little at a time, feeling the texture of the mix regularly. When it is ready it will be like large loose breadcrumbs that will come together as a dough if you squeeze them between your fingertips. You may not need to use all the eggs, or you may need to add a little more.

Tip the mixture out onto a floured surface and push together, then knead until it forms a dough. Wrap in cling film and leave to rest for several hours before rolling and cutting as required.

BRAISED CANNELLONI

SERVES 🐔 🐔 🐔 🐔 🐔 🐔

olive oil
6 chicken thigh or leg portions
10 small shallots, chopped
10 plum tomatoes, chopped
100g pitted black olives
10 pasta sheets 20-25cm x 15cm
300g large leaf spinach, stalks
　removed
100g butter
10g nutmeg, freshly grated
200g mascarpone
salt and pepper

Heat a little oil in a casserole. Season the chicken, add to the pan and cook until well coloured. Add the shallots and cook for a few minutes. Add the tomatoes and olives and transfer to the oven for 1 hour. When done, let the chicken cool a little before stripping the meat from the bones and stirring it back into the sauce. Scoop out the sauce solids with a slotted spoon so that you have a thick stew for filling the pasta and a thin sauce to bake the cannelloni.

Cook the pasta sheets in a pot of boiling salted water for 3 minutes if using freshly made pasta, or according to the packet instructions. Refresh in cold water. Meanwhile, in a large saucepan, cook the spinach in the butter, stirring constantly until it has just wilted. Season with nutmeg, salt and pepper. Let the spinach cool, then mix it with the mascarpone and spread the mixture out in the bottom of a baking dish.

Heat the oven to 200°C (gas 6). Spoon a generous amount of the chicken mixture along the middle of each pasta sheet, adding a little more seasoning. Roll up and cut each roll into two cannelloni. Stack all the cannelloni on top of the spinach and pour the thin sauce over. Place the whole lot in the oven and bake for 30 minutes. Serve sprinkled with olive oil.

DUCK RAVIOLI

SERVES 🐔🐔🐔🐔🐔🐔

600g pasta dough (page 216)
1 egg, beaten
1 red chilli, deseeded and sliced
2 spring onions, chopped
1 small bunch coriander leaves

FILLING
1kg duck legs
olive oil
2 carrots, chopped
1 onion, chopped
1 celery stick, chopped
60g galangal, chopped
1 garlic clove, crushed
1 star anise
50ml port
200ml red wine
500ml chicken stock (page 20)
4 tbsp dark soy sauce
4 tbsp fish sauce
salt and pepper

BROTH
1 duck carcass or bones
   leftover from a roast duck
2 tbsp fish sauce
50g ginger, sliced
1 lemongrass stalk, peeled and
   chopped
2 star anise
1 small handful coriander
   roots, chopped
1 tbsp dark soy sauce
1/2 tsp sesame oil

This is a very complex dish but rewarding to make.

Heat the oven to 190°C (gas 5). To make the filling, trim any excess fat from the duck legs and season well. Heat a little oil in a frying pan, add the duck and fry until well browned on all sides.

Heat some more oil in a casserole and add the vegetables, galangal, garlic and star anise. Cook until the vegetables are just soft. Add the port and red wine and boil until reduced to a glaze. Add the duck legs and stock and bring to the boil, skimming. Add the soy and fish sauces then transfer to the oven and cook for 1 hour, or until the duck is very tender.

Meanwhile, make the duck broth. Put all the ingredients in a pot with 2 litres water, bring to the boil and simmer for about 1 hour.

Put the pasta dough through a pasta machine following the manufacturer's instructions. Cut the dough into 12 circles about 10cm in diameter and keep them covered with cling film until you are ready to fill them.

Take the duck from the oven and keep the legs warm. Strain the liquid, put it back in the pan and bring to the boil. Keep bubbling until you have a thick sauce. Meanwhile, shred the duck and mix it with the sauce.

Place a spoonful of duck in the centre of half the pasta circles. Brush the edges with egg and press the remaining circles on top. Pinch around the edges to seal well.

Bring a large pan of salted water to the boil and add a dash of oil. Working in two batches, cook the ravioli for about 4 minutes (they will be done 2 minutes after they float to the surface).

Meanwhile, strain the duck broth into a warmed serving bowl. As the ravioli cook, put them in the broth. Serve garnished with chilli, spring onion and coriander.

CHICKEN LAKSA

SERVES

250g thick noodles
250g fish balls
vegetable oil
250g very large prawns
200g can coconut milk
1.25 litres chicken stock
1 tsp fish sauce
250g chicken breast, cubed
50g choy sum, thinly sliced
50g beansprouts
25g cucumber, julienned
1 bunch coriander, chopped
a little chilli powder
sambal oeleck, to serve

LAKSA PASTE
½ tsp coriander seeds
1 pinch cumin seeds
1 onion, chopped
50g ginger, peeled and chopped
5 coriander roots
1 lemongrass stalk, peeled and
   chopped
4 lime leaves, chopped
50g candle nuts or blanched
   almonds
1 tsp shrimp paste
4 garlic cloves
1 tsp ground turmeric
1 tsp ground coriander
2 tsp ground cumin
2 large red (serrano) chillies,
   deseeded and chopped
100g red curry paste

Buy a ready-made laksa paste if you don't want to make your own. Asian supermarkets sell ready-made fish balls too.

Cook the noodles following the packet instructions, then drain and keep in a warm place. Meanwhile, fry the fish balls on all sides in a little oil and set aside. Shell and devein the prawns.

To make the laksa paste, toast the coriander and cumin seeds in a dry pan until they release their aromas and colour slightly. Combine in a food processor with the onion, ginger, coriander roots, lemongrass, lime leaves, nuts, shrimp paste, garlic and 20ml vegetable oil and blend to a purée.

Heat 100ml oil in a large pan and add the turmeric, ground coriander and cumin, and the chillies. Fry for about 5 minutes, stirring all the time, until fragrant. Add the spice purée to the pan and cook, stirring continuously, for 5 to 8 minutes, until you have a very aromatic jam-like paste. Set aside.

Meanwhile, heat a little oil in a wok and fry the red curry paste for about 10 minutes, until the paste darkens. Add the laksa paste and let them bubble together until dark and aromatic. Add the coconut milk, chicken stock and fish sauce and bring to the boil. Add the prawns, chicken and fish balls and cook for 5 minutes.

Pour the hot sauce into big serving bowls, then add the noodles. Garnish with the choy sum, beansprouts and cucumber. Sprinkle with chopped coriander and a little chilli powder. Serve the sambal oeleck separately in a small bowl for people to help themselves. If they are your friends, warn them if you've chosen a blow-your-head-off type!

PHAT THAI

SERVES 🐔🐔🐔🐔

600g thick dried flat rice
    noodles (banh pho)
3 chicken breast fillets
100ml vegetable oil
100g garlic cloves, finely
    chopped
1 bunch coriander, roots
    separated and leaves picked
20 medium-sized prawns,
    peeled and deveined
150g pickled turnip, chopped
30g sugar
4 eggs, beaten
50ml fish sauce
20ml oyster sauce
600g beansprouts
1 bunch spring onions, cut
    diagonally
100g roasted peanuts, crushed
3 red chillies, deseeded and
    finely chopped
1 lime, quartered

Phat Thai (pronounced pad Thai) is central Thailand's greatest snack food, sold at hawker markets within Bangkok and the many towns that surround it. Phat Thai is never very spicy; the chillies are added at the end, usually by the consumer. For me the special ingredient is pickled turnip, which gives the sour dimension and crunchy texture that makes the best phat Thai. Add the lime at the last minute – if it cooks it becomes bitter.

Soak the rice noodles in cold water for up to 2 hours then drain and keep to one side. Cut the chicken into long thin strips slightly thicker than the noodles.

In a wok, heat the oil over a high heat. When shimmering, add the garlic and coriander roots and stir for a few moments. Add the chicken, prawns and pickled turnip and cook for 30 seconds. Add the sugar, then the eggs and cook for another 30 seconds. Stir in the fish sauce and oyster sauce. Add the noodles and toss for approximately 2 minutes.

Add the beansprouts and spring onions and toss well. Put the noodles in a serving dish and finish with picked coriander, roasted peanuts, chillies and wedges of lime.

TURKEY SOUP NOODLES WITH WATER CHESTNUTS

SERVES

50g ginger, peeled
50g garlic, peeled
50g coriander roots, plus a few
   coriander sprigs, leaves
   picked
400g turkey escalopes
vegetable oil
700g thick Chinese wheat
   noodles, or udon
100g sugar snap peas
220g can water chestnuts,
   drained and sliced
50ml soy sauce
100ml kecap manis
150ml Thai fish sauce
1.5 litres chicken stock (page 20)
100g beansprouts
salt and pepper

Pound the ginger, garlic and coriander roots together to make a paste and set aside.

Heat a griddle until very hot. Rub the escalopes with oil and season with salt and pepper. Chargrill on both sides until cooked through, then cut the turkey into fine strips and set aside.

Meanwhile, heat some oil in a hot wok. When it is shimmering, add the ginger paste and stir until fragrant. Add the noodles and stir-fry for about 2 minutes. Add the sugar snaps and the water chestnuts. Toss well and cook for another minute. Add the soy sauce, kecap manis and fish sauce and cook for 2 minutes. Tip in the stock and bring to the boil.

Ladle the noodle mixture into serving bowls. Top with the turkey, beansprouts and picked coriander and serve.

CHICKEN AND SAKE NOODLES WITH EGG AND SPRING ONIONS

SERVES

3 chicken breast fillets, skin on
200g spring onions
50ml vegetable oil
100g ginger, finely julienned
50g garlic, very very finely
    sliced
600g straight-to-wok udon
    noodles
400ml sake
3 eggs, beaten
50ml soy sauce

Bloody quick and bloody delicious. Udon noodles are the big fat soft white ones from Japan.

Cut the chicken breasts into strips about 2cm wide and the full length of the breast then set aside. Cut the spring onion into pieces the width of your thumb, keeping the white and green parts separate.

Heat a wok and add the oil. Once the oil is hot, add the chicken followed by the ginger and garlic and stir-fry for 2 minutes until the chicken is just coloured. Add the whites of the spring onions and stir-fry briefly before adding the noodles and the green parts of the spring onions. Toss for a couple of minutes so the noodles heat through.

Pour in the sake and the wok should boil. Stir then add the beaten eggs. Add the soy and stir well. When the egg is just starting to cook, remove the wok from the heat and stir so the egg finishes cooking in the residual heat.

DUCK SOUP NOODLES WITH SCALLOPS & GINGER

SERVES

BROTH

1 Chinese roast duck (page 174)
5g Sichuan peppercorns
10g ginger, sliced
15g star anise
10g spring onions
10g cinnamon sticks
250ml soy sauce
150ml Shaoxing wine
100g yellow rock sugar
50ml sesame oil
5g garlic cloves, sliced

GARNISH

1kg wonton noodles
500g scallops
200g root ginger, peeled and
   cut into matchsticks
200g spring onions, sliced
   diagonally
150g pea tops or snowpea
   shoots

Strip the meat from the duck and set aside. Chop the carcass into four or five pieces. Put the carcass in a pot, cover with about 4 litres water and bring to the boil. Simmer for 10 minutes, skimming as necessary, then reduce the heat to a low simmer. Add all the remaining broth ingredients and continue simmering for 1 hour.

Meanwhile, bring a pot of water to the boil, add the wonton noodles and cook according to the packet instructions. Drain and keep the noodles warm by covering them with cling film. Slice or shred the duck meat.

When the stock is ready, strain it into a clean pan and adjust the seasoning to taste.

Cut the scallops crossways so that they are the thickness of a pound coin. Put a heavy frying pan over a high heat and sear them for 30 seconds on each side.

Divide the noodles, scallops and duck meat among serving bowls. Pour in the broth and scatter with the ginger, spring onions and pea tops before serving.

GRILLED PARTRIDGE WITH BLACK CABBAGE AND POLENTA

SERVES

1 large onion, sliced
100g butter
350g cavolo nero (Tuscan black cabbage)
100g cep or chestnut mushrooms
20g parmesan, shaved
50ml oil
12 partridge breasts
6 rosemary branches
seriously delicious olive oil
salt and pepper

POLENTA
300ml milk
1 garlic clove, crushed
100g polenta
120ml double cream
20g parmesan cheese, grated
70g mascarpone

Char the breasts well so they are slightly bitter and provide a real contrast to the sweet, salty polenta and spicy cabbage. You can also serve this as a starter.

Start with the polenta. Put 200ml water in a saucepan with the milk, garlic, salt and pepper and bring to a rolling boil. Add the polenta, stirring constantly in a clockwise direction, and keep stirring until the mixture thickens and comes back to the boil. Reduce the heat to very low and cook, stirring very frequently, for 45 minutes. Add the cream and parmesan cheese and continue cooking over a low heat for another 10 minutes, until the cheese has completely dissolved. Remove the pan from the heat and stir in the mascarpone. Keep warm.

Meanwhile, heat the oven to 180°C (gas 4). In a heavy frying pan, fry the onion gently in the butter. Strip the leaves from the stems of the cavolo nero and boil for 10 minutes in heavily salted water. Drain and set aside. Add the mushrooms to the onion and season well. Add the cavolo nero and cook gently for 15 minutes.

Put a griddle pan over a high heat to get really hot. Meanwhile, spoon the polenta onto heatproof serving plates, top with the mushroom mixture and scatter with parmesan shavings. Place in the oven for 10 minutes while you cook the partridge.

When the griddle is searing hot, open the windows as you are about to create a lot of smoke (alternatively you can cook the partridge on the barbecue). Oil and season the partridge breasts and lay them skin-side down on the griddle. Place the rosemary on top and cook for 3 minutes then turn, placing the rosemary back on top. Transfer the griddle to the oven for 5 minutes (or continue cooking on the barbecue, turning every 2 minutes so both sides of the partridge have two goes at the heat).

Serve the partridge with the polenta and vegetables and a drizzle of your fabulous olive oil.

CHICKEN BIRYANI

SERVES

300g basmati rice
25g butter
1 large onion, finely sliced
1 bay leaf
3 cardamon pods
1 small cinnamon stick
1 tsp turmeric powder
4 chicken breast fillets,
   without skin, cut into large
   chunks
100g hot Indian-style curry
   paste
1 handful raisins
1 litre chicken stock (page 20)
1 large handful chopped
   coriander
1 large handful toasted flaked
   almonds

Wash the rice three times and set aside to drain. Heat the butter in a saucepan and cook the onion with the bay leaf, cardamon and cinnamon for 10 minutes. Sprinkle in the turmeric, then add the chicken and curry paste and cook, stirring, until aromatic.

Add the rice and raisins and continue cooking and stirring for a good few minutes. When fragrant, add the stock and bring to the boil. Cover with a tight-fitting lid and once it starts to boil vigorously, reduce the heat and cook for 10 minutes.

Turn off the heat but don't lift the lid on the pan. Leave the biryani to sit for 20 minutes. Just before serving, stir in half the almonds and coriander, then serve with the rest of the almonds and coriander thrown over the top.

CHICKEN AND WILD GARLIC RISOTTO

SERVES 🐓🐓🐓🐓🐓🐓

15g butter, plus 40g for
  finishing
1 tbsp olive oil
4 shallots, diced
4 garlic cloves, crushed
300g chicken thigh fillets, cut
  into chunks
350g arborio rice
900ml boiling chicken stock
  (page 20)
100g parmesan cheese, grated
40g butter
1 large handful wild garlic
  leaves, torn

No one likes chalky, undercooked rice, so when making risotto it is important that the stock and rice are a similar temperature, so that the heat doesn't fall when you add the stock. If it does, the rice may not cook properly.

Wild garlic leaves are around for a short period only in spring. Look for them in good markets or ask your greengrocer to get some for you. Be careful as they are a lot stronger than they look. If you can't get wild garlic, try a mix of soft herbs, such as sage, basil, chives and chervil.

Heat the butter and oil in a large, heavy pan. Add the shallots and cook until just translucent, then add two of the garlic cloves and the chicken and cook for another 3 or 4 minutes. Add the rice and stir for a couple of minutes to coat the grains.

Have your pan of boiling chicken stock at the ready. Add a couple of ladles of stock to the rice and stir with a spatula until all the liquid is taken up and the rice is scraped from the bottom of the pan. Keep adding ladles of stock, stirring and scraping all the time, to avoid sticking. After about 15 or 20 minutes the rice grains will be tender but still firm to the bite and the risotto mixture will be creamy and moist.

Add the parmesan and remaining butter and whip with a wooden spoon to put more air into the risotto. Throw in the wild garlic leaves and serve immediately.

CHICKEN PAELLA

SERVES 🐓🐓🐓🐓🐓🐓

120ml olive oil
2 white onions, diced
4 garlic cloves, crushed
4 over-ripe tomatoes, chopped
100g chorizo, sliced
1 red chilli, chopped
30 saffron strands
400g paella rice
600ml vegetable stock
1 red onion, diced
200g mussels
100ml white wine
300g large peeled prawns,
   deveined
300g chicken breasts, without
   skin, cut into pieces
100g green beans
1 tsp smoked paprika
1 large handful coriander
   leaves
salt and pepper

Nearly every traveller to Spain has experienced a paella – some good, some not so good depending on the freshness of the ingredients, the care taken with the seasoning, and the speed at which it is served. The quality of the rice is important – look for a bag with grains that are whole, with none broken.

Heat a paella pan (or large wok), add 60ml olive oil then the white onions. Cook gently for 3 to 4 minutes. Add the garlic and cook for 1 minute, then add the tomatoes, chorizo and chilli. Increase the heat and add 20 saffron strands followed by the rice. Cook for 3 to 4 minutes. Pour in the stock and bring to the boil. Reduce the heat to a simmer and cook, stirring occasionally so it doesn't stick and burn.

Meanwhile, heat 60ml oil in a large casserole over a very high heat. Add the red onion and fry for 2 minutes, then throw in the mussels. Pour the wine over the top, stir well and leave to cook for 5 minutes, stirring occasionally.

Add the prawns and chicken – but be gentle. Add the beans, smoked paprika and ten saffron strands. Stir again and place a well fitting lid on top. Cook for 3 minutes until the prawns change colour and all the mussels are open (discard any that don't open). Check the beans are not too crunchy.

By now the rice should be cooked, so add half the chicken-seafood mixture to it and stir. Add the coriander to the remaining chicken-seafood mixture and spoon it into the middle of the paella. Take the pan to the table, open a good bottle of rioja and share with your friends.

If you can master a few great dishes and think it is time to really become a great cook, learn the art of preserving. Confit, terrines, sausages, pastrami – all are foods that have traditionally been put aside for winter when there is little in the way of fresh produce.

A great cook utilizes everything and does not buy a chicken breast in a pack but buys a whole bird and bones it out. The legs of that bird, if then cooked and stored in fat as the recipes here show, are something of a miracle – soft, juicy and sweet.

The first time you make pâté it may seem a chore, but do persist. Make it a few times and you will get used to it and see how simple it really is. The game terrine is the most difficult and time-consuming recipe here, but you will clearly taste the difference. Never again will you go to the deli and ask for a slice of their stuff.

I love pastrami and want more people to make it so the whole world can eat it. Turkey pastrami takes a few a days, but so what? Start Thursday and by Sunday lunch people will be eating pastrami with bagels and pickles, their mouths agape that you – yes you! – made it. The bonus is that these treats will keep in your fridge for a good week or more – that's economical.

confit, terrines,
pâtés & pastrami

CONFIT DUCK

SERVES 🐔 🐔 🐔 🐔 🐔 🐔

6 cumin seeds
12 coriander seeds
3 juniper berries
1 garlic clove, sliced plus
  1 whole head garlic, halved
100g sea salt
6 duck leg and thigh joints
1 small bunch thyme
1 rosemary branch
about 500g duck or goose fat
2 bay leaves
1 tsp black peppercorns

The fat used to make the confit can be reused over and over, the flavours improving every time.

The day before cooking, put the cumin and coriander seeds in a dry pan and toast until they are slightly coloured and aromatic. Remove to a board and crush them with the blade of a knife. Crush the juniper berries and sliced garlic clove as well and mix the spices with the salt. Rub the mixture over the duck, scatter with thyme, rosemary and sliced garlic and leave for 24 hours, turning two or three times as they marinate.

Next day, wipe the duck with kitchen paper and pat dry but don't wash off the marinade. (The salt extracts the water from the meat cells, which will be reinflated with fat as the duck cooks gently. If you wash it, you will simply reinflate the cells with water.)

Put the duck in a cast-iron casserole and cover with the goose or duck fat. Add the bay leaves and peppercorns. If you have the time to keep an eye on the oven, I find that slowly raising the temperature to a peak and then reducing it steadily helps to keep those cells filled with fat. I start at 150°C (gas 2) and raise the temperature by 20°C every 15 minutes for 45 minutes, then reduce at the same rate for a further 45 minutes. Otherwise, cook the whole lot at 170°C (gas 3) for 1 hour 30 minutes, until the meat is almost falling off the bone.

You can store the duck very simply by placing it in a pudding bowl, covering it with the fat and keeping it in the fridge: as long as it stays covered with fat it will last for weeks.

CONFIT DUCK WITH HARICOT BEANS, SAUSAGE AND PANCETTA

SERVES 🐓🐓🐓🐓🐓🐓

350g dried haricot beans, soaked overnight in cold water
1 carrot, chopped
1 onion, chopped
4 tomatoes, chopped
1 bouquet garni
2 sprigs flat-leaf parsley
2 sprigs sage, plus extra sage leaves to serve
4 tbsp olive oil
125g pancetta, cut into thin lardons
200g toulouse sausage, sliced
4-6 confit duck legs (page 234)

If you want to cheat, ready-made confit duck can be bought in jars from good supermarkets and speciality delicatessens.

Drain and rinse the soaked beans, then put them in a large saucepan and cover with cold water. Add the vegetables, herbs, olive oil and pancetta and bring to the boil. Simmer for 1 hour, or until the beans are soft. Drain off the excess liquid, discarding the bouquet garni and herb sprigs. The beans should have the texture of a thick soup. Add the sliced sausage and heat through.

Meanwhile, heat the oven to 180°C (gas 4). Remove the confit duck legs from their fat. Put an ovenproof frying pan on the stove until it is hot. Add the duck legs skin-side down and cook for 4 minutes. Turn the legs and transfer the pan to the oven for approximately 20 minutes.

Pour the bean mixture into shallow bowls and sit a piece of duck on top. Garnish with sage leaves.

CONFIT CHICKEN WITH
MASH AND GREEN SAUCE

SERVES

2 cardamon pods
12 coriander seeds
3 juniper berries
100g sea salt
1 small bunch thyme, leaves
  picked
1 whole head garlic, halved,
  plus 1 clove garlic, crushed
6 chicken leg and thigh joints
about 500g duck or goose fat
pared rind of 1 orange
pared rind of 1 lemon
2 bay leaves
1 small bunch rosemary
1 tsp black peppercorns
mashed potatoes (page 157)
  and salsa verde (page 66), to
  serve

Tip: confit rabbit legs are absolutely delicious and only need a slightly longer cooking time than chicken. You can confit pheasant legs too, in which case follow the cooking times for confit duck as pheasant has a more fibrous musculature than chicken and the meat will take longer to reach tenderness.

This is all about soft moist chicken legs served with great buttery mash and a tart but herby rich sauce.

The day before cooking, put the cardamon pods and coriander seeds in a dry pan and toast until they are slightly coloured and aromatic. Remove to a board and crush them with the blade of a knife. Crush the juniper berries as well and mix the spices with the salt, thyme and crushed clove of garlic. Rub the mixture over the chicken and leave for 24 hours, turning two or three times as they marinate.

Next day, heat the oven to 150°C (gas 2). Wipe the chicken with kitchen paper and pat dry but don't wash off the marinade. Put the chicken in a cast-iron casserole and cover with the goose or duck fat. Add the halved garlic heads, orange and lemon rinds, bay leaves, rosemary and peppercorns and place in the oven for 10 minutes. Increase the heat to 180°C (gas 4) for 15 minutes, take it up to 200°C (gas 6) for another 15 minutes, then 230°C (gas 8) for about 10 minutes. Check the fat is bubbling, then start to reduce the heat: 200°C (gas 6) for 15 minutes, 180°C (gas 4) for another 15 minutes, then switch off the oven and leave for another 10 minutes or so, until the meat is almost falling off the bone. Alternatively, cook the whole lot at 170°C (gas 3) for 1 hour. Serve with mashed potatoes and salsa verde.

CHICKEN LIVER PÂTÉ

SERVES

500g chicken livers
300g softened butter
400g bacon, diced
3 onions, diced
2 tbsp brandy
freshly grated nutmeg
clarified butter, to cover
  (optional)
salt and pepper

Good old pâté is so simple to make though few people will ever think it. Give it a go and just chuck everything in – I do!

Check the chicken livers for any greenish stains and cut them off as even as a scrap will make the pâté bitter. At the same time, pull each lobe away from its connecting threads.

Heat 100g of the butter in a non-stick frying pan until just foaming. Add the bacon and the onions, season well and cook for 8 to 10 minutes or until the onions are soft and the bacon is thoroughly cooked. Add the livers and fry quickly until cooked but still quite soft in the middle, about 2 minutes.

Increase the heat. Add the brandy and carefully ignite it with a match, tilting the pan to spread the flames across the livers. Add a little salt, pepper and grated nutmeg and remove from the heat.

Transfer the mixture to a food processor and blend. For a smooth finish, press the pâté through a coarse sieve as well. Return the pâté to the food processor and blend in the remaining 200g butter. Check the seasoning then press the pâté into a ceramic crock or individual pots and chill well.

The surface of the pâté will gradually oxidize – that is, it will darken in contact with the air. If you wish to avoid this, cover the pâté with a thin layer of clarified butter once it's in the pot/s.

DUCK LIVER TERRINE

SERVES

1 onion, finely chopped
3 garlic cloves, finely chopped
500g butter
6 peppercorns
6 bay leaves
6 thyme sprigs
300ml dry white wine
vegetable oil
700g duck livers, cleaned so
    free of any green bits
200g duck foie gras, chopped
2 eggs
30ml madeira
30ml port
30ml cognac
freshly grated nutmeg
salt and pepper

Line the base of a 1kg terrine (I use a Le Creuset terrine) with greaseproof paper. Cook the onion and garlic without colouring in a frying pan in a little of the butter and some oil. Add the peppercorns, bay leaves, thyme and white wine. Bring to the boil and let it reduce to a syrup.

Put the duck livers, foie gras and eggs in a food processor and blend to a paste. Push the purée through a very fine sieve into a large mixing bowl.

Meanwhile, melt the remaining butter in a saucepan and bring to the boil. In a separate small pan, boil the madeira, port and cognac until reduced by half, then add to the hot butter. Strain the onion and wine mixture into the butter as well, pressing down to extract all the flavours, then discard the solids. Stir the boozy butter and liver mixtures together until combined. Season with nutmeg, salt and pepper.

Heat the oven to 150°C (gas 2) and pour the mix into the lined terrine. Lay a tea towel in the base of a roasting tin and sit the terrine on top. Pour 500ml water around the terrine, making a bain-marie. Cover with a lid or foil and cook for 25 to 30 minutes. Remove from the oven and leave the terrine to cool for a few hours before turning it out.

DUCK RILLETTES

SERVES 🐔🐔🐔🐔🐔🐔🐔🐔🐔🐔

500g duck leg and thigh joints
500g belly pork, cut into strips
3 tsp sea salt
10 garlic cloves, chopped
3 thyme sprigs, leaves picked
1 tsp ground black pepper
500g-1kg goose or duck fat

This is yum – and really bad for you if you can't eat fat!

The day before cooking, rub half the sea salt into the duck legs then layer in a container with half the garlic and thyme. Do the same with the pork. Cover and leave in the fridge overnight.

Next day, heat the oven to 160°C (gas 3). Remove the meat from the fridge and rub off the salt, garlic and thyme. Place in a casserole and cover with goose or duck fat. Bring to the boil then transfer to the oven for about 2 hours.

Strain the meat, reserving the fat. When it is cool enough to handle, but still warm, flake the pork and keep to one side. Do the same with the duck, making sure there are no bones. Shred the skin finely.

Mix the pork and duck together well, add the pepper and salt to taste. Gradually add about two-thirds of the strained goose or duck fat and mix well until the rillettes is the consistency of mayonnaise.

Check the seasoning (it needs to be well seasoned) then place in little pots, or two big pudding bowls in 1970s style, and cover with the remaining fat. Chill until set.

GAME TERRINE

SERVES

6 pigeon breasts
400g lardo
600g boneless chicken
1kg duck and/or chicken livers
100g boneless partridge and/or
  pheasant
250g boneless duck breast
1 tbsp chopped garlic
1 tbsp allspice powder
1 tbsp chopped parsley
3 tbsp armagnac
375ml dry white wine
200ml concentrated stock
onions madagascar, to serve
  (page 246)
salt and pepper

This recipe is half-nicked from Marco Pierre White when he was cooking at Harvey's – that's why it's more opulent than most other terrines. Don't skip the marinating process or the result will be dry and have little flavour.

Two days before serving, cut all the meat into 1cm-sized pieces, putting all the best pieces to one side. If the pigeon breasts are quite small, leave them whole. From the best bits, weigh out 175g lardo, 260g chicken, 450g livers, 75g duck, and all the pigeon and partridge or pheasant.

Mince all the remaining meat and fat and add the garlic, then half each of the allspice, parsley, armagnac and wine. Season the cubed meats and sprinkle with the remaining allspice, parsley, armagnac and wine. Place both mixes in the fridge overnight.

Next day, heat the oven to 180°C (gas 4). Combine the minced meat mixture and concentrated stock, then stir in the chopped meats. Press into a well-greased 1kg terrine, packing down well.

Cover tightly with greaseproof paper and then foil. Lay a tea towel in the base of a roasting tin and sit the terrine in it. Surround the terrine with as much warm water as possible without spilling. Place in the oven and reduce the heat to 160°C (gas 3). Bake without opening the oven door for 1 hour and 15 minutes. Remove the terrine from the oven and leave it to cool in the tray of water for 1 hour.

Take the terrine from the water and weigh the contents down with a something like a big book. Leave in the fridge overnight. Keep the juices that leak out: they will be gelatinous and can be chopped and served alongside the terrine.

Next day, turn the terrine out and slice it. Serve with chutney (recipe follows), plus pickles, salad and lots of crispy hot toast.

ONIONS MADAGASCAR

SERVES

2 tsp olive oil
500g small round shallots
70ml vinegar
1 tsp sugar
100g tomato purée
50g raisins
1 bay leaf
2 thyme sprigs
1 handful chopped parsley

This is properly made with shallots rather than onions. Shallots have more than one bulb inside the skin, whereas onions are single bulbs – so that'sha lot. However if you can't find shallots, pickling onions will work just as nicely here. The acid in the pickle cuts through the fat of pretty well any terrine.

Heat the oil in a saucepan and sauté the shallots until they are just coloured. Add the vinegar and sugar and cook until brown, then add the tomato purée and raisins.

Add all the herbs and 125ml water. Sit a lid on the saucepan skew-wiff, and simmer very gently until the shallots are soft, about 35 to 40 minutes. The longer and slower the cooking, the more intense the flavour will be, and if you leave it to sit in the fridge for a day before serving, the flavour will improve further.

Also good with onions madagascar: rillettes ♥ pâtés ♥ smoked fish ♥ salads made with confit chicken ♥ buffet foods

SMOKED DUCK SALAD WITH ORANGE AND FENNEL

SERVES 🐓🐓🐓🐓🐓🐓🐓🐓

100g soft brown sugar
100g lapsang souchong tea
  leaves
1 handful couscous or rice
4 duck breasts
salt and pepper

SALAD
1 large fennel bulb
1/2 lemon
2 oranges, peeled and sliced
50ml olive oil
1 small bunch dill, picked

You can buy smoked duck – and smoked chicken – from decent delis but here is a quick and effective means of smoking at home. The salad is worth serving on its own too. Once smoked, duck breasts will last about a week.

Line a wok with a sheet of foil. Mix together the brown sugar, tea leaves and couscous or rice and spread evenly around the base of the wok. Sit a rack in the wok. Score the duck skin, season with salt then place the duck skin-side up on the rack and cover with a tight-fitting lid.

Turn the heat under the wok to high: after about 10 minutes it will start to smoke. Leave the wok on the stove for another 15 minutes, then remove from the heat and leave to smoke for 15 minutes more.

Lay the smoked duck skin-side down in a cold frying pan and place over a high heat. Leave it for 6 to 7 minutes, so the fat melts slowly and skin becomes crisp. Turn the duck breasts over and remove the pan from the heat. The skin should be crisp, the flesh lean, and the flavour of smoke should run all the way through the meat. Leave to cool.

To make the salad, shave the fennel, sprinkle with salt and squeeze the lemon juice over. Add the oranges and olive oil, but don't stir through the dill until just before serving.

Slice the duck very thinly lengthways, spread it out on serving plates and scatter the salad over.

TURKEY PASTRAMI

MAKES 800G
50g whole black peppercorns,
  plus 1 tbsp extra
1 large handful crushed
  juniper berries
2 tbsp coriander seeds, crushed
200g soft brown sugar
150g sea salt
6 garlic cloves, crushed
2 tsp thyme leaves
1 tsp whole cloves
3 bay leaves
2 small turkey breasts,
  400g each

SMOKE
100g soft brown sugar
100g lapsang souchong tea
  leaves
1 handful couscous or rice

Variation: you can smoke the pastrami in the barbecue instead. Combine 300g green wood chips, 250g tea leaves and two handfuls of rice and place the mixture on a sheet of foil. Lay it over the glowing coals, cover and smoke as above.

I love the American deli scene, where turkey pastrami is a classic. However it's hard to buy in Britain so here is a recipe. It takes a few days but is seriously delicious.

Whiz 50g black peppercorns in a small food processor or blender until they are crushed, then tip them into a fine sieve and shake gently. You need to sieve the crushed peppercorns twice: the kibble that is left over is for the pastrami. Combine the kibble, juniper and coriander seeds and set aside.

In a saucepan combine 500ml water with the brown sugar and salt. Bring to the boil, stirring until the salt and sugar have dissolved. Remove from the heat and stir in 1 tablespoon whole black peppercorns, plus the garlic, thyme, cloves and bay leaves. Leave to cool.

Place the turkey breasts in a big plastic container and pour the cooled brine over it, making sure the turkey is completely covered. Chill for 48 hours.

To smoke, line a wok with a sheet of foil. Mix together the brown sugar, tea leaves and couscous or rice and spread evenly around the base of the work. Sit a wire rack on top.

Remove the turkey from the brine, rinse under cold water and pat dry with paper towels. Cover the turkey with the pepper and juniper rub, pressing it into the surface.

Lay the turkey skin-side down on the rack, cover and smoke for about 2 hours, until it has cooked all the way through. Remove from the smoker and leave to cool. The turkey will continue to gain flavour the longer you let it rest – wrap it tightly in cling film and refrigerate up to 1 week.

Slice the turkey and serve with lots of gherkins, mustard, some endive and sliced soft bread with lashings of mayonnaise.

DUCK PASTRAMI WITH MUSTARD SAUCE

SERVES

200g soft brown sugar
150g sea salt
1 tbsp whole black
  peppercorns
6 garlic cloves, crushed
2 tsp thyme leaves
1 tsp whole cloves
3 bay leaves
800g duck breasts
1 large handful crushed
  juniper berries
2 tbsp coriander seeds, crushed

SMOKE
100g soft brown sugar
100g lapsang souchong tea
  leaves
1 handful couscous or rice

MUSTARD SAUCE
300ml single cream
300ml dijon mustard

In a saucepan combine 500ml water with the brown sugar and salt. Bring to the boil, stirring until the salt and sugar have dissolved. Remove from the heat and stir in the peppercorns, garlic, thyme, cloves and bay leaves. Leave to cool.

Place the duck breasts in a big plastic container and pour the cooled brine over them, making sure the duck is completely covered. Chill for 24 hours.

To smoke, line a wok with a sheet of foil. Mix together the brown sugar, tea leaves and couscous or rice and spread evenly around the base of the work. Sit a wire rack on top.

Remove the duck from the brine, rinse under cold water and pat dry with paper towels. Mix together the juniper and coriander and rub all over the duck, pressing it into the surface.

Lay the duck skin-side down on the rack, cover and smoke for about 30 minutes, until it has cooked all the way through. Remove from the smoker and leave to cool. The duck will continue to gain flavour the longer you let it rest – wrap it tightly in cling film and refrigerate up to 1 week.

To make the mustard sauce, put the cream in a heavy saucepan, bring it to the boil and boil until the volume of liquid has reduced by half. Use a whisk to beat in the mustard, then remove the pan from the heat. Serve the sauce with the sliced smoked duck.

POULTRY & GAME DEALERS

RETAILERS

ALLEN & CO
117 Mount Street,
London W1K 3LA
Tel 020 7499 5831
www.allensofmayfair.com

ANGUS FARM SHOP
42 Main Street,
Greyabbey, Newtownards,
County Down BT22 2NG
Tel 028 4278 8695

ANDREW ARMSTRONG FARMERS & BUTCHERS
The Square, Bakewell,
Derbyshire DE45 1BT
Tel 01629 812 165

DOVE'S BUTCHERS
71 Northcote Road,
London SW11 6PJ
Tel 020 7223 5191
www.doveandson.co.uk

FURNESS FISH, POULTRY AND GAME
Moor Lane, Flookburgh,
Grange-Over-Sands,
Cumbria LA11 7LS
Tel 01539 559 544
www.morecambebayshrimps.com

RT HARVEY PURE MEAT
63 Grove Road, Norwich,
Norfolk NR1 3RL
Tel 01603 621 908

KENT & SONS
59 St John's Wood High Street,
London NW8 7NL
Tel 020 7722 2258

C LIDGATE
110 Holland Park Avenue,
London W11 4UA
Tel 020 7727 8243

DJ MACDOUGALL
Canal Side, Fort Augustus,
Inverness-shire PH32 4AU
Tel 01320 366 214

KENNETH MORRISON
Strath, Gairloch, Ross-shire
IV21 2BZ
Tel 01445 712 485

M MOEN & SONS
24 The Pavement,
London SW4 0JA
Tel 020 7622 1264

PICKARDS BUTCHERS
74-78 Carlisle Street, Goole,
East Yorkshire DN14 5EP
Tel 01405 761 433

CH WAKELING
41 Farncombe Street,
Godalming, Surrey GU7 3LH
Tel 01483 417 557
www.wakelings.co.uk

MF WOOD
51 Hartopp Road, Clarendon
Park, Leicester LE2 1WG
Tel 01162 705 194
www.mfwood.co.uk

WYNDHAM HOUSE
2 Stoney Street, London SE1 9AA
Tel 020 7403 4788

FARMS, FARM SHOP/STALLS AND ONLINE SALES

ADAMS POULTRY
100 Cooley Road,
Six Mile Cross, Omagh,
County Tyrone BT79 9DH
Tel 028 8075 8223

BAKEWELL DUCKS
Charlton Farm,
Hartlebury, Kidderminster,
Worcestershire DY11 7YE
Tel 01299 250 206

BLACKFACE
Crochmore House,
Irongray, Dumfries,
Dumfriesshire DG2 9SF
Tel 01387 730 326
www.blackface.co.uk

BLAGDON FARM SHOP
16-18 Milkhope Centre,
Blagdon, Newcastle-upon-Tyne,
Northumberland NE13 6DA
Tel 01670 789 924
www.theblagdonfarmshop.co.uk

CALDECOTT'S HOLLY FARM
Batemans Lane, Wythall,
Worcestershire B47 6NG
Tel 01564 829 380

CHANCTONBURY GAME
North Farm, Washington,
Redhill, Sussex RH20 4BB
Tel 01903 877 551
www.chanctonburygame.supanet.com

COPAS TRADITIONAL TURKEYS
Kings Coppice Farm, Grubwood
Lane, Cookham, Maidenhead,
Berkshire SL6 9UB
Tel 01628 474 678
www.copasturkeys.co.uk

EAVES GREEN GAME FARM
Goosnargh, Preston,
Lancashire PR3 2FE
Tel 01772 865 300

GOODMAN'S GEESE
Walsgrove Farm,
Great Witley, Worcester,
Worcestershire WR6 6JJ
Tel 01299 896 272
www.goodmansgeese.co.uk

HEAL FARM
Kings Nympton, Umberleigh,
Devon EX37 9TB
Tel 01769 572 839
www.healfarm.co.uk

KELLY'S TURKEYS
Springate Farm, Bicknacre
Road, Danbury, Essex CM3 4EP
Tel 01245 223 581
www.kelly-turkeys.com

MADGETT'S FARM FREE RANGE
Tidenham Chase, Chepstow,
Gwent NP16 7LZ
Tel 01291 680 174
www.madgettsfarm.co.uk

MANOR FARM GAME
Long Grove Wood Farm, 234
Chartridge Lane, Chesham,
Buckinghamshire HP5 2SG
Tel 01494 774 975
www.manorfarmgame.co.uk

QUAIL WORLD
Penrhiwllan, Llandysul,
Pembrokeshire SA44 5NR
Tel 01559 370 105

SELDOM SEEN FARM
Billesdon, Leicester,
Leicestershire LE7 9FA
Tel 01162 596 742
www.seldomseenfarm.co.uk

SHEEPDROVE ORGANIC FARM
Warren Farm, Sheepdrove,
Lambourn, Berkshire RG17 7UU
Tel 01488 674 747
www.sheepdrove.com

WOODFORD MEATS
Bolt Hall Farm,
Larkhill Road, Canewdon,
Rochford, Essex SS4 3SA
Tel 01702 258233
www.woodfordmeats.co.uk

INDEX

DEDICATION
To the wonderful memories of my Nanna Foley

It's one of those things with acknowledgements that, should you mention someone and it is not enough, it is not enough, and should you not mention someone then you're doomed. This project started life as a book on game birds and water fowl and is now one that specialises in the humble chicken. This I sometimes battle with, but I hope that you get great enjoyment from all the work that has gone into it by so many very talented people. Firstly, to the ever-patient and very wonderful Aussie who even under the effects of jet-lag can function and is the best editor in all the world: Miss Jenni Muir – you rock and are bloody cool.
To all at Quadrille for taking the risk with me and this great book – especially to Claire Peters for standing, watching and turning this into a thing of beauty, and to Anne Furniss, many thanks. A really big thank you to all the people at Smiths and THE LUXE who cook, trial, test and toil – and just for being fab. To Tony Moyse – so cool and a great cook – and to Jason Lowe for his lovely work. Also a big thank you for those who I've forgotten or maybe just missed out on purpose!

Editorial Director Anne Furniss
Creative Director Helen Lewis
Project Editor Jenni Muir
Designer Claire Peters
Photographer Jason Lowe
Production Director Vincent Smith
Production Controller Ruth Deary

First published in 2009 by
Quadrille Publishing Limited
Alhambra House
27-31 Charing Cross Road
London WC2H OLS
www.quadrille.co.uk

This edition first printed in 2013

Text © 2009 John Torode
Photography © 2009 Jason Lowe
Design and layout © 2009 Quadrille
Publishing Ltd

The rights of the author have been asserted.All rights reserved. No part of this book may be reproduced, stored in a retrieval system or transmitted in any form or by any means, electronic, electrostatic, magnetic tape, mechanical, photocopying, recording or otherwise, without the prior permission in writing of the publisher.

Cataloguing in Publication Data: a catalogue record for this book is available from the British Library.

ISBN 978 184949 321 5

Printed in China